AND THE
BRIDGE
IS LOVE

The Reuben/Rifkin
Jewish Women Writers Series
A joint project of the Hadassah-Brandeis Institute
and the Feminist Press

*Series editors: Elaine Reuben,
Shulamit Reinharz, Gloria Jacobs*

The Reuben/Rifkin Jewish Women Writers Series, established in 2006 by Elaine Reuben, honors her parents, Albert G. and Sara I. Reuben. It remembers her grandparents, Susie Green and Harry Reuben, Bessie Goldberg and David Rifkin, known to their parents by Yiddish names, and recalls family on several continents, many of whose names and particular stories are now lost. Literary works in this series, embodying and connecting varieties of Jewish experiences, will speak for them, as well, in the years to come.

Founded in 1997, the Hadassah-Brandeis Institute (HBI), whose generous grants also sponsor this series, develops fresh ways of thinking about Jews and gender worldwide by producing and promoting scholarly research and artistic projects. Brandeis professors Shulamit Reinharz and Sylvia Barack Fishman are the founding director and codirector, respectively, of HBI.

OTHER BOOKS IN THE
REUBEN/RIFKIN SERIES

Shalom India Housing Society
by Esther David

Hold On to the Sun
by Michal Govrin

Dearest Anne: A Tale of Impossible Love
by Judith Katzir

If a Tree Falls:
A Family's Quest to Hear and Be Heard
by Jennifer Rosner

Arguing with the Storm:
Stories by Yiddish Women Writers
edited by Rhea Tregbov

Dream Homes:
From Cairo to Katrina, an Exile's Journey
by Joyce Zonana

FAYE MOSKOWITZ

AND THE BRIDGE IS LOVE

LIFE STORIES

**THE
FEMINIST PRESS**
AT THE CITY UNIVERSITY
OF NEW YORK
NEW YORK CITY

I wish to thank my friend and editor, Deanne S. Urmy,
for the resonance her order brings to my work.
And thank you to my late professor and mentor,
A. E. Claeyssens, the bridge that spanned everything.

Published in 2011 by the Feminist Press
at the City University of New York
The Graduate Center
365 Fifth Avenue, Suite 5406
New York, NY 10016

feministpress.org

Preface copyright © 2011 by Faye Moskowitz
Text copyright © 1991 by Faye Moskowitz

Additional copyright information on page 148.

First printing 1991 by Beacon Press.
Second edition with new introduction published November 2011
First printing, November 2011

Cover and text design by Drew Stevens

Library of Congress Cataloging-in-Publication Data

Moskowitz, Faye
And the bridge is love : life stories / Faye Moskowitz. — 2nd ed., with new introd.
    p. cm.
Includes bibliographical references and index.
Originally published: Beacon Press, 1991.
ISBN 978-1-55861-770-4
1. Moskowitz, Faye. 2. Jewish women—United States--Biography. 3. Jews—
United States—Biography. I. Title.
E184.J5M74 2011
973'.04924—dc23
    [B]

12011024024

With love,
this book is for
Shoshana, Peter, Frank,
Heidi, Seth, Julie,
Elizabeth, and Jeffrey,
and for my grandchildren,
Helen Avery Grove,
Jonathan David Korns,
and
Henry Nicholas Moskowitz,
but mostly and always
for Jack.

There is a land of the living
And a land of the dead
And the bridge is love,
The only survival,
The only meaning.

—Thornton Wilder
The Bridge of San Luis Rey

PREFACE

Every other morning, our milkman in Detroit, Oscar Schwartz, a landsman, carried his wire basket straight into our kitchen and put the bottles away in the Frigidaire. Who needed the *Detroit News* or the *Free Press* when we had Oscar making the rounds of our neighborhood? Later, my mother poured off the yellow cream that rose to the top of the milk and saved it for my father's cereal and coffee. He had the ulcer, after all.

Sometimes when we were by ourselves, my mother would pause for a moment at the porcelain sink, a damp dish towel in her hand, and her eyes would seem to focus on a faraway spot, a place that filled me with loneliness; I knew she had left me then for somewhere I could not follow. I can't know if she travelled into the cloudy waters of memory or if, with a prescient shudder, she was trying to pierce her future. Always she would shake herself out of her momentary trance and come back to me. She would sigh and say, "Ay, Faygele, *dos leben is a cholem.*"

What did it mean, "Life is a dream"? As a girl, I thought my mother meant that life was "dreamy," an adjective I applied to everything good: my latest teen crush, the sentimental songs I played on my portable record player, or the happy discovery of a sweater that made me look sexy, not fat. I was even able to buy my definition for a while, for what could I understand then of past or future, so gripped was I in the pincers of the moment?

But when I was sixteen, my mother left me for a perpetual dream. I grew up quickly, married, had four children. We moved to Washington, DC, and I put Michigan behind me, or so I thought. I went to college, got my BA the year I turned forty, went on to pass my comprehensive exams for a PhD. I began to teach, and just as importantly, I started to write, mostly the ragtag contents of my dream-bag. Out they tumbled, stories that no longer served me, but were too good to give away. Not so surprisingly, I wrote of home, of the early years that shaped me, of the ghosts who peopled my dreams.

Now, twice the age my mother was when she died, I am an octogenarian, a somber mouthful that conjures up images for me of slow-moving sea creatures, dreamily floating, waving their multiple arms, at once enticing me into their grasp and stunning me with fear of the nothingness they promise.

Twenty years have passed since *Bridge* was first published. Thumbing through it today, I see Michigan everywhere. I love this book. Long-lost family and friends are preserved here as if they were put up in gleaming jars of ruby fruit, stored in a lavish pantry. Events I might have forgotten, both significant and foolish, are here, lined up on tidy shelves. Perhaps more than anything, my book is a love song to the places where I grew up, to Jackson, our exile—and to a Detroit that exists now only in dreams.

And what have I learned, fifty years away from Michigan, now that the "octogenarians" bob ever closer? Try as I might to grasp them, my memories become more dreamlike, scraps and shards drift in and out, some vivid and unforgettable, some as elusive as quicksilver, darting away like schools of gleaming fish.

I cried when I left Michigan; I couldn't have foreseen the new life that would present itself in Washington, the maturing of my children, the priceless gift of grandchildren, the deep new friendships, the teaching, the books. And who could have foretold the myriad ways we filed away our rough edges and melded our dreams, I and my beloved Jack?

Perhaps in Gan Aden, Oscar Schwartz still carries his wire basket, bottles clinking, into my mother's kitchen. Perhaps they pause for a moment to talk of family in this paradise where cream still rises to the top. Perhaps the child I was still hides in a corner, listening, listening.

I look ahead warily, and like my mother once did, seek to part the leafy branches of the future. I mourn the profligate days I wasted over the years, the precious hours set out like yesterday's newspapers; no real expectation of recycling now. My mother was right. Life is indeed a dream, and morning comes too soon. The night's uneasy wanderings melt away like spun sugar on the tongue with only a bit of sweetness lingering to recall the remarkable journey.

AND THE
BRIDGE
IS LOVE

O UTSIDE THE WINDOW OF MY daughter's old room where I lie in bed alone, the homely night scenes of my street play themselves out. The aftermath of a spring shower drips from leaf to leaf, slides down the trunks of stately trees; night birds chirp their silver chain of melody and couples coming home anticipate in easy whispers a last drink, a page or two, or the familiar comfort of making love before calling it an evening. No such closure for me; my bones intimate terminal diseases, and my heart loses time. The window curtains hang limp, all their starch, like mine, eaten away by the sodden air.

This is the room I come to nights when sleep refuses to come to me. I smoke cigarettes and eat smuggled chocolate, wrestle the *New York Times* Sunday puzzle all week for the one word that will break it open, or look at pictures of quilt patterns: "crown of thorns," "trip around the world," "rocky road to Kansas." It isn't so much insomnia that's brought me here tonight as it is washcloths.

We never have any, or at least that's what Jack says. He's been trying to get a washcloth in this house for ten years he tells me when I hand him a dampened hand towel to wash his face and hands with. When you've been married for forty years, it's convenient to argue in decades.

Jack is having an attack of sciatica, a pinched nerve, one of those supposedly humorous afflictions, like lumbago or the gout, I first learned about from comic strips: Major Hoople in his fez with pain stars radiating from his hip or Jiggs resting his bandaged foot on a little stool while Maggie brandishes her rolling pin. For four days I've been doing the stairs two at a time, bringing Jack movies from the video store and food I hope will tempt him and a king's ransom of muscle relaxers and pain relievers, none of which seem to deliver their promise. I feel terrible for him; I imagine sciatica as a kind of root canal of the hip joint, and he hurts so much my picking up the newspapers in our room makes him wince. I would do anything to make him feel better; he knows that, and I know he knows it, but it still makes me angry when he blows up at me about washcloths.

I wish washcloths were all of it. At People's, where I had the prescriptions filled, the clerk looked straight at me and said without apology, "Senior citizen's discount?" Jack and I are both frightened. What if this all just doesn't go away? A moment ago I had a fast-forward flash: he never gets better. For the rest of his life he is confined to our bedroom and an excruciating hobble across the hall to pee. I can see his beard growing out and his cheeks caving in, my world shrinking to the limitations of this house. Selfish? Isn't it Mersault's father in *The Stranger* who witnesses every execution he can find because he considers walking away from death life's greatest triumph? Is that so crazy? Don't most people leave a sick room thinking, deep down, thank God I got off this time; for the moment, at least, *I'm* still okay?

From our bedroom I can hear the radio playing softly: "Blues in the Night." A-hooey-da-hooo-ee. Jack would say this is just like me—magnify something until I've worked myself into a state, and what good does it do anyone? Well, my insomnia does someone good once in a while. When my first grandchild was born, I went over and spent the night a few times so the new parents could get some uninterrupted sleep. Getting up in the middle of the night is nothing to me. But that thin little wail, blue as skim milk, brought it all back, ripping through my sleep with the insistence of heavy muslin sheets tearing. I felt for a moment as if I were once again bent over in the rocker, cradling my own baby, and she, rooting, head bobbling, then mouth fastening onto my nipple cracked and sore, my whole body recoiling from those blind blue eyes, that first searing suck, and then my womb contracting in empathy and relief. I used to have fantasies about bombing La Leche headquarters; those smug women suckling away, while I could never get the hang of nursing at all.

Jack won't let anyone but our children come up to visit him. "I don't want people to see me like this," he says. Being sick is embarrassing to him. I don't help with the Florence Nightingale shtick, making him feel like a real invalid with my carrying of trays and recording of doses. What else can I do? Men make lousy patients; I'll bet any nurse would tell you that. Still, when I stay here in this other room I feel as if I have deserted him; when I hover, he only gets cross.

I worry I'm not sympathetic enough. I can't understand why *his* pain makes *me* feel lonely. Maybe the problem is that pain is invisible, shut up inside the person so it's impossible for another to be part of it. A gaping wound—now that would make my own flesh quiver in response. As it is, I keep looking for some outward manifestation of the hurt, have to force myself not to get into a no-win contest over pain thresholds. Meanwhile, cocooned in his misery, Jack has exiled me to this spare room.

My friend Jenny needed me sometimes in the middle of the night when she couldn't sleep. She was dying of a cancer that consumed her body like a fast-burning brush fire, and toward the end even painkillers and sleeping pills didn't help. We had signals worked out between us: she would dial my number and let the phone ring only once so as not to waken Jack. It was spring then, too. I'd throw on a raincoat over my thin cotton nightgown and go out the back door and through the neighbors' yards to her house on the next street.

I remember the beam of my flashlight and the way it grew fat when it illuminated my sandaled feet or stretched long and skinny when I pointed it ahead of me. Here or there I saw the gold medallion of an illuminated bathroom window; sometimes the Beatles throbbed on a third floor where teenagers were supposed to be sleeping. Cool green leaves brushed against my face, and the fine webs of spiders; there were no dogs living along the way, only a cat that sometimes arched its back across my legs, leaving the memory of its fur a moment on my flesh.

We didn't worry so much about intruders in those days. I had my own key and even knew the stairway well enough to avoid the third and seventh treads, the ones that might waken others who surely needed their sleep. I can't tell you what a gift it was for me to be called upon that way. I never felt more alive than in those few months Jenny let me help her die.

I came at her call one night bringing a little basket of polish and implements to do her nails. She lay curled on the edge of a king-sized bed filled with pillows of every size: European squares, neck rolls, small down-filled circles smooth as Necco Wafers. On her bedside table a half dozen pieces of perfect fruit filled a small crystal bowl that gave back lamplight in miniature, over and over. Flowers were everywhere: bouquets of peonies bending over with the weight of their bloom, crisp yellow and white tulips, a precious bunch of lilies of the valley from her own front yard, scenting the room like dime-store perfume.

This was still a feminine room despite white enamel basins and collections of pills and capsules in childproof caps; the woman in the bed steadfastly insisting on remaining a woman, not merely a patient. Her bright blue-and-green-flowered nightgown slipped from shoulders where the flesh now stretched taut as canvas prepared for a painting. Her eyes were closed when I tiptoed in, trying to compose myself, trying to think of something to say that would not be trivialized by her drama. "How was your day? What's new?" Even the talk we call "small" seemed bathed in irony.

"I feel just awful," she said without opening her eyes. "Sit here on the bed next to me. Don't talk. Just hold my hand." Her pulse threaded under my palm. "What can I do for you?" I said at last, and when she didn't answer I picked up a heavy wooden hairbrush and smoothed her hair. Over and over I pulled the bristles through the still-gleaming black strands. "Such beautiful hair," I crooned, petting her, caressing the wasted arms, the bent shoulders, the submissive back.

I said, "Look what I've brought you," and spread the little bottles and tools on a nearby table. One by one, I filed her waxy-colored nails into almond shapes, chose from the assortment the sauciest red I could find, and made of each nail a defiant flag. "Don't move," I said as if she had somewhere to go. She spread her fingers on the coverlet, her gypsy coloring, always so vivid, almost garish now that her cheeks glowed faintly yellow under her tanned skin.

Ours was a recent friendship though I had known about her for years: an artist, what I would call a patrician, with her impeccable WASP credentials, her prominent husband—just the kind of person whose acquaintance my reverse snobbery would keep me from pursuing. Merely comparing her upbringing to mine made me feel like someone just out of steerage, a bundle in one hand, a squawking chicken in the other.

But we did meet, at the home of a neighbor who knew us both, and in fifteen minutes over coffee Jenny and I discovered correspondences only women in their late forties will admit to; by the time we agreed to lunch the next day on egg salad sandwiches at the People's on Wisconsin, we were anticipating the kind of deep, new friendship each of us had stopped expecting long before. For about two years after that we saw each other almost every day, commiserated about our teenagers, laughed about the gray in our hair (the dread badge of courage) but refused to cover it, took classes together at GW and drank coffee in the student union, talking politics and gossiping about favorite professors with classmates half our age.

I never stopped being surprised that she had chosen me. Her house, crowded with upholstered evidence of old money, still left me tongue-tied, and I changed clothes four times before I got the courage to walk over and meet her mother one day, a shriveled woman in a wheelchair, my childhood dictionary definition of "dowager."

I was in my kitchen the morning Jenny called me from the doctor's office. "It's cancer," she said, almost in amazement, "the galloping kind. There's no hope, darling." I held my breath, and the protective shutters slammed down like those formidable barricades in front of little shops in France. What did that mean, "no hope"? Who said the word "cancer" out loud? What kind of doctor told patients they had nothing to pray for? This was the gentile world with a vengeance: stiff upper lip where my people would have rent their clothing, howled about the injustice—and consulted another doctor. But secretly I shuddered with a kind of relief. Lightning doesn't strike in the same place twice. Perhaps my own body would be safe for a little while. We talked second opinions; I hung up the phone and wept.

"There's one more thing you can do for me," Jenny said, cupping her fingers so she could blow her nails dry. "I'm dying for a shower." She rolled her eyes. "Joke," she said, and then, "Do you think you could help me?" She drew her legs up and pulled herself to a sitting position, biting her lower lip until it was pale between her teeth. Outside, on Newark Street, an automobile passed, radio blaring. "Please," she said. "Sponge baths just won't do it. I would feel so much better if I could only get under the water."

She saw my reluctance. Did I really want this responsibility? What if she stumbled, or fainted in the tub? For a moment I was struck by an absurd shyness; our 2:00 a.m. assignations seemed suddenly juvenile to me, something kids might do, not two grown women, one of whom was dying. Jenny pushed the blankets behind her. "You can't hurt me, you know. I'm past all that."

I put my arms around her waist and held her in front of me while we inched forward to the hallway, stopping every few feet for her to catch her breath. Each flaw in the polished wood floor, even the metal strip that anchored the hall carpeting, presented an obstacle. By the time we reached the bathroom, we were both sweating. While I steadied her, Jenny reached down, gathered up the silk hem of her gown, and drew it over her head.

It was clear I needed to turn my face from her as much to preserve my own privacy as hers, but Jenny was too close to me in that small room, her nakedness palpable, something I couldn't avoid, no matter where I looked. If Jenny noticed my hesitation, she didn't acknowledge it. "Quick," she said, hugging her elbows, swaying. "Help me!"

I sat her down on the closed toilet seat and adjusted the faucets so the shower ran a gentle blood warm. Then, taking her under the armpits, I half lifted, half dragged her into the tub. When she was standing under the spray, I pulled the plastic curtain over my body between us, partly to shield myself from some of the water, and partly because it was one more way to define myself as separate from her, another way of saying that when all this was over, I could walk away from her dying.

"Are you okay?" I kept saying. Steam fogged the window and the mirror and beaded the toilet and sink. Water ran down the arm with which I held Jenny and began to soak my cotton gown. "This is heaven," she said, lifting her face to the stream. "I wish I could stand here forever." And I thought, these are the elements to which we are finally reduced. After the refusal to believe, after the wrenching leave-takings and the resignation, come the small gifts freshly seen. Days before, I had cooked young carrots, no bigger than a thumb, and brought them to her in a pale blue bowl. We both cried when she licked the crumbs: another spring, all she was leaving—a smear of buttery sweetness on her fingers.

No way to stay dry and I hadn't the heart to call an end to the bathing just yet. On an impulse, I stripped off my dripping gown and stepped into the tub with her. As she leaned her back into my body, I shampooed her thick hair with sweet-smelling soap and let the water plaster the strands against her head. I soaped her neck and shoulders, down her arms and then the backs of her legs, which had begun to tremble from fatigue under my hands.

Later we sat drinking tea in her room, our heads wrapped turban-style in white terry towels, Jenny back in bed and I, wearing one of her robes, in a chair nearby. She was exhausted, her bit of hoarded energy expended, spilled like sugar from a cloth sack. I said, "Jenny, I'm sorry. I shouldn't have let you do this. You'll be a wreck today." But all the while I kept thinking of my father, on his deathbed, refused the cigarette that had become his final shamefaced request. "They're bad for you, Daddy," I had told him, still pretending at the very end. I wish now I had given him that smoke; what difference would it have made to anyone but him?

When Jenny's hair was dry, she lay back against the pillows, as if asleep. The room was so quiet I could hear someone in another part of the house murmur in a dream. Through trees in full leaf, the sky, starless, appeared as patches of blue enamel. "I never knew it would be so hard," Jenny said, turning her head to me, eyes still closed. "Hard to die, you mean?" She opened her eyes for a moment and looked straight at me. "Hard to keep on living," she said.

And now, in the spare room, I dream I am embracing a lover, whether man or woman, I do not know. On my back for the moment, I look up at the high ceiling that seems to shoot through the roof, and see, staring down at me, the face of a beautiful young girl. Her hair is the bright yellow of school crayons and frames her face in a scrawl of curls. Even though she is made small by distance, I can clearly see that the girl's eyes are blind-blue like a newborn's, and her arms, which appear suddenly as objects do in dreams, move with the slow thoughtful motion of underwater plants. Centuries pass before the girl realizes what she is witnessing. I feel as if my lover and I are at the bottom of a deep well and the girl is peering over the rim at us. Eons more before it occurs to me that orientation is everything; perhaps the situation might actually be reversed, perhaps all this time *I* have been looking down the long cool cylinder at *her*.

This afternoon, when I brought him lunch, Jack said, "What would I do without you? What do sick people do who are all alone?" This is the way he tells me he loves me, and remembering that now, I go back to our own room and crawl gingerly into bed beside him, where I lie very still, my knees grazing his back, trying not to cause him any more pain.

W<small>E ARE TALKING NOW OF</small> remembering, that random weeding out of experience so that what remains stands in relief like the drama of vivid blossoms freed from the distraction of undergrowth. Looking back, we perceive that a pattern has emerged as though the years were a bolt of color unfurling from the loom, weft and warp intricately, inextricably intertwined, already established in spite of the artist whose life itself creates the art. We call these designs memory.

Memory can chalk in childhood with the pastels of nostalgia—or cut like a whiplash into the face of sentimentality. Memory is a miner's lamp braving our journey down into darkness. For each of us, the journey back is as personal and convoluted as the whorls of an individual fingerprint. But as memory is not linear, it has no single beginning or end. Flash a moment on a remembered scrap of nursery wallpaper, and suddenly a world returns: the creaking rocker; the breast, sticky and sweet; the face of your mother, safely young; and the song she learned years before those years, wrapped in her own mother's arms.

Try as we might to shuck them off, the memories of childhood remain, strapped to our backs like bundles we are charged to carry always. We bear these burdens so long they become part of us, so familiar we forget, sometimes, their contents, but our shoulders round to their shape even when we think we have momentarily set their weight aside.

Memory is idiosyncratic, at once impish and implacable. What are we to do, for instance, with the unbidden specters that invade our nights, as the imprint of a searing sun floats, ghostly, before our eyes long after we have entered a darkened room? And how do we crack the mind's code when the desired image refuses to surface to the screen? What can we do but take on our ghosts, sift our memories, forego beginnings—a shifty word where personal time is concerned. We will want the patience of the artisans who lined the winding streets of old Saint Paul de Vence with flowers made of stones, the courage to taste our fathers in a smudge of ash. And the medallions of memory—sun-struck—will come.

Today we live in the midst of an electronic age. As the pace of life picks up more and more quickly, memory seems sometimes as fractured as the ephemeral images with which we are constantly bombarded. From the grainy newsreels of our youth to the ubiquitous (and disposable) television footage that now chronicles our days and ways, the visual has come to dominate our senses. All the more precious then, the words caught between covers, words that tell us how it was to be alive at a certain time in history. As the stage manager says in Thorton Wilder's *Our Town*, "This is the way we were: in our growing up and in our marrying and in our living and in our dying."

For who will testify, who will accurately describe our lives if we do not do it ourselves? The world, our personal one and the world that roils outside us, is in constant flux—each moment that occurs, no matter how seemingly insignificant, each shifting grain of sand, makes the second that has just passed history. Yet we have our roots in that evanescence and are constantly transformed by it. Once something has been set loose in the world, it permeates the very air we breathe. We cannot be unaffected by what has gone before; we recapitulate history, our own and the world's, each time we draw breath. And as we document our days, the preservation of what has gone before is earnest of our faith in what's to come.

"JEWISH CHRISTMAS"—THAT'S what my gentile friends called Chanukah when I was growing up in Michigan in the thirties and forties. Anachronistic, yes, but they had a point. Observing the dietary laws of separating milk and meat dishes was far easier for the handful of Jewish families in our little town than getting through December without mixing the two holidays.

Christmas was a miserable time for Jewish children in those days; nothing short of quarantine could have kept us from catching the Christmas fever. My parents were no help. Immigrants who had fled pogroms in Russia and Poland, they were world-class outsiders. If tee shirts with mottos had been in fashion then, our shirts would surely have read Keep a Low Profile. My mother would never have considered going to my school to complain about the Christmas tree in the lobby or the crèche in our principal's office or the three life-size wise men, complete with camels, that we cut out of construction paper in Art and hung on our classroom walls.

If I still wasn't convinced Christmas was coming after all those reminders, I had only to look at the advent calendar hanging behind my teacher's desk or walk downtown, where carols blared out over loudspeakers and built to a crescendo in front of the six-foot neon cross decorating our largest department store. And as for keeping a low profile, try it when yours is the only neighborhood house in work clothes while every other is dressed for a party.

By the time we moved to the Jewish section of Detroit, I was old enough to accept Christmas as a holiday other people celebrated. Chanukah was our winter holiday, not a substitute at all, but a minor-league festival that paled before Passover, Rosh Hashanah, and Yom Kippur. All the cousins gathered at our grandparents' house where we lined up to get Chanukah gelt from the uncles: quarters and half dollars, and dollar bills, perhaps, for the older children. Mostly we ran around a lot, got very flushed, and ate latkes, plenty of them.

My own children were raised in a diverse neighborhood in Washington, DC. The Ghost of Christmas Past clanked its chains for a while, and my husband and I learned to make a few concessions. Still, we never sunk to the Chanukah bush or an actual Christmas tree, though we knew Jews who did; we lit the menorah, bought presents for each of the eight nights, decorated our house with blue and white paper chains, and played with dreidels. In spite of all that, our kids were pretty disgruntled for most of December, although even their non-Jewish friends had to concede we had something with those latkes.

For the past few years, with our children grown, my husband and I have cut off the Chanukah/Christmas debate entirely. We distribute the Chanukah gelt early and then leave the country. That's going to a lot of trouble to avoid office parties and the eggnog and pfeffernuss for which we never did develop a taste, but at least we don't have to get caught up in the general depression that afflicts not only the people who celebrate Christmas but all the rest who don't and wish they did.

Several years ago, we found ourselves in Venice during the holidays. In spite of all our rationalizations, we missed being home with our children, missed the ritual of lighting the menorah, the tacky paper chains, the dreidel game we play, gambling for raisins or nuts; and at that moment we would have traded any pasta dish, no matter how delectable, for potato latkes like the ones we ate at Chanukah as far back as we both could remember.

So maybe that's why, with the help of guidebooks and our faltering Italian, we threaded our way through the city's bewildering twists and turns until we suddenly emerged into a spacious square that marks the old Jewish ghetto of Venice. The clip-clop of our heels on cobblestones and the flutter of pigeons punctuated a silence that might have existed for centuries or only on that particular rest day, we didn't know. "There's an old synagogue at the other end of the square," my husband said. "Let's go see if maybe it's open for visitors." We pulled at the heavy brass-studded wooden door, and far down a long corridor I heard the sound of many voices chattering in Italian. "I'm probably hallucinating," I whispered to my husband, "but I swear I smell latkes."

In that musty, crumbling building, the memories flooded back as clear as the icicles we licked in those nose-numbing December days of my Michigan childhood. Bundled against the stunning cold, we walked hand in hand, my mother and father, my brothers and I, along darkened streets where orange candles in brass menorahs bravely illuminated each front window we passed.

In my grandparents' vestibule, we shed our snowy boots. The welcoming warmth of the coal furnace promised more coziness deep inside; there my aunts sucked in their bellies as they elbowed past one another in and out of Bobbe's tiny kitchen, from which they pulled a seemingly endless array of delicious dishes as if from a magician's opera hat: platters of bagels slathered with cream cheese, smoked fish with skins of iridescent gold, pickled herring, thick slices of Bermuda onion strong enough to prompt a double-dare, boiled potatoes with their red jackets on, wallowing in butter. Best of all were the crisp potato latkes, hot from Bobbe's frying pan, to eat swaddled in cool sour cream, the contrasting textures and temperatures indelibly printing themselves on our memory.

Though our mothers' cooking styles were virtually interchangeable, my husband and I used to quarrel every year about whose family made the better latkes. My mother's potato pancakes were thin and lacy, delicate enough to float in their hot cooking oil. His mother's latkes, I pointed out at every opportunity, utterly lacked refinement: colossal, digestion-defying pancakes the size of hockey pucks, they were each a meal in themselves. "Just the way I like them," my husband would tell me as he wolfed yet another one.

I never learned to make my mother's latkes. She died just before my husband and I were married, and when we came to Washington we brought my mother-in-law with us, so her potato latkes won by default and became part of our children's Chanukah tradition. Which is not to say I ever accepted them graciously, and as we moved into our middle years, and cholesterol moved into our lexicon, my husband, too, scorned the latkes of his childhood. "The Israeli secret weapon," he called them when his mother wasn't listening. "Eat two, and you're on sick call for at least a week."

But friends came each Chanukah and brought their children to celebrate with ours. We exchanged small gifts: boxes of crayons, pretty bars of soap, cellophane bags of sour candies for Grandma, who, of course, supplied the latkes. Early in the afternoon, she would begin grating potatoes on a vicious four-sided grater, the invention of some fiendish anti-Semite who must have seen the opportunity to maim half the Jewish population each December.

The trick was to finish grating just before the guests arrived so the potatoes would not blacken, as they have a discouraging tendency to do. Meanwhile, as she mixed in eggs, matzo meal, salt, and baking powder, Grandma heated a frying pan with enough oil to light the Chanukah lamps into the next century. The finished latkes were drained on supermarket paper bags that promptly turned translucent with fat. Still, we ate them: great, golden, greasy, dolloped-with-sour-cream latkes, and our complaints became part of our Chanukah tradition, too.

The Venetian latkes didn't taste very much like Grandma's, but there was enough resemblance to quell our homesickness. Well, that was a while ago. Today, though November leaves, red and brown and gold, still hang on stubbornly, the Christmas drumming has already begun. My morning's *Washington Post* bursts with ads like a ripe pomegranate spewing seeds. Overnight, green wreaths have sprouted on our neighbors' doors, and the Salvation Army kettle, come out of storage, stands on its tripod in front of the Giant food store once again. I remember how little I cared for this time. For a moment, the buried stones of jealousy and of shame and not belonging work themselves to the surface with a speed that surprises me.

But this year something is different; suddenly, finally, *I* am the grandma who makes the latkes. Two little grandchildren, both named for my mother-in-law (may she rest in peace), will come to our house to watch us light the menorah. Baby Helen at two and a half can already say the Hebrew blessing over the candles, and if my joy in that could translate to Chanukah gelt, all the banks in America would be forced to close.

I close my eyes and think of Grandma tasting a bit of her childhood each Chanukah when she prepared the latkes as her mother had made them before her. My mother, my aunts, my own grandmothers float back to me, young and vibrant once more, making days holy in the sanctuaries of their kitchens, feeding me, cradling me, connecting me to the intricately plaited braid of their past, and even at this moment, looking down the corridor of what's to come, I see myself join them as they open their arms wide to enfold my children and grandchildren in their embrace.

ONE OF MY EARLIEST RECOL-
lections is of a tall white picket fence at the back of a yard
that must have belonged to a house we lived in when I
was a child. I write this sentence and realize already how
skewed my vision was. "A tall fence," I say, but tall to
whom? If I was three or four at the time, it might have
been an ordinary little fence such as many homes were
surrounded by in the thirties, scarcely higher than the
head of a tiny girl.

So the memories of childhood must always be seen
in a perspective different from that of an adult's eye. The
knothole through which I watched the comings and
goings of a pretty blonde lady, a blonde man with a mus-
tache, and a small girl like myself limited my vision as
sharply as my yet unfolded years. From time to time, one
of the neighbor people drifted in and out of my narrow
field of vision like a bird that perches momentarily on
a trembling tree limb and then, unaccountably, is lost
from sight.

Many of my earliest memories are mysteries I probably will never solve now that those who might have explained them to me are gone. I fall back on experience and intuition, build my fragile cardhouse of speculation, and hope my solutions are not ridiculously far from the mark. What am I to make, for instance, of the certainty with which I remember hearing that my grandfather never spoke to his sister again after she married a non-Jew? Was it true that he sat shivah for her, said the prayers of mourning for her, considered her dead?

With such unforgiveness in my consciousness, was it any wonder that years later, when my own daughter told me she was marrying a gentile, I went into a depression that couldn't be lifted until the memory was dragged out and reckoned with. Never mind that my future son-in-law was a splendid young man my family had known since he was a boy. Forget that I thought I had long ago distanced myself from the obdurate orthodoxy that now swept back to envelop me in a wash of shame and guilt. No rationalization could free me from the image of my grandfather's sister, startlingly alive, beating on the lid of the pine coffin in which my young imagination had once so securely confined her.

For weeks after my daughter's announcement I grieved inside unable to explain my complicated feelings to myself, let alone to those near to me. Outwardly

I moved ahead, considering the myriad decisions even a small wedding entails. Only when I began searching for the rabbi I insisted would marry the couple did I realize how unyielding was the wall of law and tradition surrounding me. I wasn't naïve enough to consider an Orthodox rabbi, but I thought perhaps a Conservative clergyman might understand my desperation and help me. Intellectually, I knew we weren't entitled to the rituals of a Jewish wedding; emotionally, I wasn't prepared to relinquish them. Perhaps in my controlling way I was being as stubborn as my grandfather had been, but I knew that including my daughter and her groom in a Jewish ceremony was opting for life, while my grandfather, however reluctantly, however sorrowfully, had chosen exclusion and death. I kept calling rabbis. Phone call after phone call brought stony refusal, but finally, through that grapevine parents like myself have set up, I heard of a Reform rabbi, chaplain at one of the local universities, who agreed to perform the service provided he be able to counsel the prospective couple.

For a few days after that, the stone on my heart lifted; my daughter and I began to discuss menus, dresses, music. Even the bride and groom's vegetarianism struck me as a stroke of good fortune: those relatives who kept kosher would find plenty to eat at our wedding. I dreamed of the chuppah we would create to hold over the couple like the folds of a tent, like soft wings. A friend offered to do the calligraphy for a *ketubah*, the traditional wedding contract. We selected favorite readings from the Old Testament, poems and song lyrics.

But six weeks before the wedding, when the time came for out-of-town invitations to be sent, my depression deepened once more. I felt as if I were publishing the news of my failure as a Jewish parent. If I had only done this or that differently, I reasoned, my daughter would not now be marrying a gentile. Try as I might to put the idea out of my head, I couldn't help feeling I was breaking faith with those Jews who had perished in the Holocaust. The statistics were clear: what Hitler could not accomplish one way, intermarriage would achieve in another. The ceremony I fought for suddenly seemed a sham, a self-conscious parody of a Jewish wedding, and I had been crazy to think I could carry it off.

I kept most of my feelings to myself; I didn't want to spoil the wedding with my unhappiness. Besides, it wasn't as though ours was the first intermarriage in our extended family. I dropped invitations in the mail and hoped some of my relatives might make the trip to Washington to be with us. But my aunt and my uncles on my father's side, heirs to my grandfather's strict adherence to Jewish law, presented another problem. Again and again I looked at the tentative guest list and the question marks beside their names. I didn't know which was the greatest insult, to invite them or not to invite them, and so I did nothing.

One day when the time for the wedding could be measured in days, I placed a call to my Orthodox aunt in Michigan. "Tante," I said, "I suppose you have heard that Shoshana is getting married, so you probably know her husband-to-be is not Jewish." Once again, the depth of my inchoate shame and sadness surprised me. My aunt spoke after a long silence. "What do you want me to do?" she asked. "You know your uncles can't come to this wedding."

Suddenly I realized that this was the heart of the matter. I grieved because I wanted my daughter and her young man to exchange vows for the future in the palpable presence of their past. A new marriage represents the possibility of tomorrow, but my aunt and uncles could bear witness to the continuity of yesterday. Although my father was not longer alive, a bit of his spirit could grace our celebration if someone from his family came to be with us. I said, "Tante Frieda, I understand how you feel, but I don't want to have this wedding without you."

On a warm, sunny day in November, a blessed reprise of summer, my daughter and son-in-law were married under a lace canopy in the living room of our home. Surrounding the couple, so close that some could reach out and touch them, were their parents, a grandmother, their brothers and sisters, aunts and uncles, cousins, and friends. My grandfather's sons, my father's two brothers, stayed away; given my memories of their father, I understood. But one of the guests that day was my elderly aunt, who set aside her religious convictions against intermarriage to honor an even more basic tenet of universal faith: the love and preservation of family.

Through the knothole of my memory, I see my grandfather in his tall black yarmulke, stiff-necked, a stand-in for God, turning an implacable back on his own blood. My tunnel vision allows me little sense of what that decision cost him. But years later, the mother of four children dearer to me than life itself, I know I have another choice. I welcome the partners of my children into the home that is now as much theirs as if they had been born to me.

I will continue to live my life as a Jewish woman, mindful of the undergirdings of Torah: "Thou shalt love thy neighbor as thyself." From the time our children were old enough to understand anything so complex, my husband and I have tried to teach them the intrinsic worthiness of all people regardless of their formal beliefs. "Judge others by how they live their lives," we've said in every way we know how. And so they have. I pray the example their father and I have set for them will keep our children close to us and to each other and to the faith that can and must stretch to embrace their choices.

I KEEP PHOTOGRAPHS IN A LARGE suit-box under my bed, certain the way people are that I will mount them someday in albums, classify them by date and place. Meanwhile, they curl and fade, the writing on their backs turns lilac, and I tell myself, when I think about it, that if I do not hurry, one day there will be no one to name the thousands of images, smiling or grave, staring out of the glossy paper.

I have one photograph of my cousin Esther. She faces the camera pensively, the sun making an aureole of the hair she bleached blonde that year. For the picture she wears a white sweater and a single strand of pearls. Even in 1945, when she was sixteen, Esther had achieved a timeless elegance that makes people select the photo out of a welter of others and ask, "Who is she?"

Esther charted maps for me of exotic places my green imagination would take years to recognize. She taught me the cruel deception of appearances—how a treacherous undertow can wait under waters calm as the skin on a morning cup of cocoa, how toeholds can exist on seemingly unscalable rock. But by the time my mind and body were in sufficient concord to follow her blazes, she was no longer there, no longer dancing just ahead of me.

I think I was always a little afraid of her, all of us cousins were. She had a temper that flared without warning like a phosphorus match that blows up and singes your thumbnail when you aren't expecting it. We attributed it to her red hair, so different from the ordinary shades of brown and black we all seemed to be stuck with. And she was skinny, too, and bit her nails like the girl in the ads did before the cartoon mother with the worry vees in her forehead found Ovaltine.

When Esther came to stay with us in Jackson during the summers we were little girls, the way all the Detroit cousins did at one time or another, I discovered that my mother was afraid of her, too. Esther held her nose when she was thirsty and said Jackson water stunk like rotten eggs. Of course, I had heard that one before; I told her Detroit water was full of clothes bleach, but my mother didn't say a word when Esther refused to eat strawberry jello for dessert. "I'm not allowed to eat this stuff," Esther said. "Jello is made from unkosher cowbones." By that time I was not only ashamed of our water supply, but my mother and I both knew that Esther had found us out. She saw how we had let the ropes of religious ritual go slack, as people do sometimes when they move away from family and experience tries belief. She saw how easy it is to compromise when observance becomes a matter of conscience rather than convention. She saw and, being Esther, she would tell.

At night we undressed quickly with our backs to one another, upstairs in my bake oven of a bedroom, the June bugs banging away against the screens, and I would already feel homesick in my very own room, thinking that Esther would want me to come visit her in Detroit; I hadn't the nerve to tell her I missed my mother when I hadn't even gone yet.

We'd lie in bed and giggle and talk until my dad yelled upstairs for us to go to sleep, and we'd be quiet for a moment and then laugh some more. We cousins disagreed about Esther; some of us called her swell, but the braver among us said she was a snot. Still, no one disputed her claim to second sight; somehow Esther always knew the exact moment my father would lose patience, put down his paper, and start for the stairs. Then all of a sudden she would yawn and tell me, "It's time for prayers." That was the part I hated most. She would declare in her redheaded authoritative tone, "The second we're done, we can't say another single word or it's a sin." She prayed out loud, continuing long after I had finished my one puny little prayer. As soon as she said "amen," she carefully pulled her nightgown down over the underpants she said it was a sin not to wear to bed. When she turned her back to me and left me alone, I could almost feel her stubborn lips clamped shut, could barely distinguish her heartbeat from mine.

Suddenly, in the dark silence, the outside world would enter my room: the death rattle of an old Ford, strangers murmuring on the street, an insistent mosquito, whining, waiting. That was the time when worry climbed in bed with me full of hindsight about the day, warnings for tomorrow. I was afraid to go to sleep, but there was no arguing with Esther about what was or was not a sin. Being a rabbi's daughter, she had a direct line to God, and I knew it, so she snookered me into terrified silence every time.

Esther had crazy eating habits, like so many scrawny kids. When we were allowed to go to the ice cream parlor for a malt, Esther carried an egg with her in a little brown paper bag blown up and twisted at the top so the egg would not break. You can imagine how she walked then, taking tiny mincing steps with the little sack held out in front of her. The soda jerk always made a production of cracking the egg one-handed, letting it drop into the frosty metal container from about a foot above it. My mother laughed when I asked for an egg for my malt. She pinched the back of my tree-trunk thighs and turned away without a further answer.

One summer Esther came with her own supply of Fleischmann's Yeast, as if Jackson had no grocery stores and was truly the hick town the Detroit cousins all claimed it was. She was skinnier than ever and my mother vowed to fatten her up, assuming the task was as easy as plumping the Thanksgiving turkey we penned in the coal bin and fed stale bread and cracked corn before the holiday. The brisket our family loved so much, so tender it fell into succulent strips before it could be cut, made Esther gag. She pushed the meat around on her plate and picked out bits of fat she pronounced disgusting when she and I were alone. Noodle kugel upset her stomach, she played with her mashed potatoes, and even my mother's feathery cinnamon rolls, still steaming, she pronounced "too rich." "It's that mooshed-up yeast she eats," my mother grumbled, looking with satisfaction at my potbelly. "Thank God, I don't have any trouble with you."

What did my mother know, with her accent so thick you could spread it like peanut butter and her Old Country ways? I became convinced that Esther's asceticism and strict adherence to Jewish law fostered her slender bones and redhead's milky skin. I loathed my plump body, over which I seemed to have lost all vestiges of control, and shut my eyes to the changes that were taking place in front of them until Esther told my mother one day, "For heaven's sake, Aunt Sophie, buy her a brassiere!"

I felt certain I had only to get closer to Esther and I would absorb her secret; perhaps there was still time to throw away the old design, shape my limbs to a different set of plans. Gentile Jackson had become my adversary, but perversely I found myself daily swallowing more of my Jewishness, hiding it, until the secret seemed to blow me up as with the telltale contours of an unwanted child. Expertly twirling on a round stool at Woolworth's, I ate forbidden BLTs, toasted, and when my classmates insisted that Chinese waiters were lepers who dropped finger bones into the chop suey, I turned up my nose the way Esther might have done and told bald-faced lies about how often my family ate at the Fairy Gardens.

As if breaking the Sabbath with Saturday matinees were not sin enough, I came home after the movies and cut, and tore, and pasted, and made a great show of sitting on my front porch embroidering in cross-stitch on small, stamped squares of linen. My most hideous secret I kept to myself, a cache of religious tracts picked up from store counters around town, New Testament readings I puzzled over at night by the light of a street lamp that lit a corner of my bedroom. Of course I hadn't the nerve to do any of these things in front of Esther; I could never admit how seductive "fitting in" had become or how convinced I was that the Jewish God I still so deeply believed in was going to strike me dead after He had tired of playing with me. That summer of the Fleishmann's yeast, my mother sent me to Detroit to stay with Esther until school started. And I was ready to go. For the first time in months, I began sleeping through the night again.

THEY CAME TO ESTHER'S HOUSE SOMETIMES, THE WOMEN, late Thursday afternoons or early Friday mornings, carrying their Shabbes chickens wrapped in liver-colored butcher paper and leaking newsprint. Then my uncle, whom even his brothers spoke of as the Rabbi, wearing as always his stern black suit, would leave his study and solemnly escort the bewigged visitor into my aunt Celia's kitchen. There she, in the middle of her own Sabbath preparations, cleared a spot on the wooden work table and carefully protected it from possible contamination with thick layers of the *Jewish Daily Forward*.

The Rabbi washed his hands while the visitor unwrapped the chicken for him to examine. "See, Rabbi, when I went to kosher the chicken, I saw this blemish on its heart," or, "What do you think, Rabbi? Look how the liver is so large and yellow." And my uncle, his tiny hooked nose slightly averted, would touch the organs with the tip of a carefully trimmed fingernail. Esther and I stood half hidden behind the pantry doorway, where I could catch underneath the scent of fresh dill and parsley from her mother's already simmering chicken soup, the visitor's rank sweat, the slightly sour stink of her yellow, waxy chicken. For a moment we were all caught in arrested motion, the woman calculating whether there was still time to get to the butcher again, anticipating the argument; Aunt Celia, dish towel or spoon in hand, stopping her work to await the decision.

I never had the courage to ask Esther if she sometimes wondered, as I did, whether her father took into account the shabbiness of a peeling handbag or a pair of shoes gone tipsy at the heels when he made his judgment. Even at twelve, I knew the purchase of another chicken would not hurt the rich women, but deep down I cheered for a positive verdict for them. I was always passionately arguing for fairness, yet I felt only disdain for the poor ones who might go without meat if the chicken were found to be unclean and therefore unkosher. Just as I worshiped Esther's power, though I couldn't define it, I was drawn to those who came in well-cut dresses and smart hats, eyes and noses like crazed porcelain under their tiny veils. Their husbands could donate sterling candlesticks and gold-embroidered Torah covers to the synagogue, while the debt-ridden sat looking into their laps when the president of the shul made yet another appeal to the congregation for money. Perhaps it had nothing to do with fairness at all; perhaps I knew already that the world lined up on the side of the powerful and I just didn't want to be caught in the wrong queue.

Like as not, the Rabbi would find the chicken kosher and, tension broken, he, Esther's mother, and the woman would laugh and talk for a few moments, the visitor's eyes darting like little birds here and there in the spotless kitchen. Once, when Aunt Celia's back was turned, one of the women lifted the lid of a cooking pot, the steam clouding her glasses so that when she dropped the lid with an embarrassed clatter and said, "Excuse me, Rebbetzin," she appeared to have no eyes at all.

But they did have eyes, these women, and Esther used to tell me she knew they talked about her mother; she heard them sometimes in the U-shaped balcony of the synagogue, whispering to one another as they skillfully followed the prayers, sitting, standing, rocking back and forth, sitting again, turning the thin, red-rimmed pages of their prayer books with moistened fingers. Esther sat with her mother and sisters in the center of the U so they could look straight down to the *bemah* or slightly ahead to the altar where the Rabbi stood.

Aunt Celia had red hair, too, the color of carrot *tzimmes* cooked in honey and darkened with cinnamon, shades deeper than Esther's; she refused to cover it with a wig the way many of the Orthodox women did, but wore it braided and twisted into a coronet like the beautiful queens pictured in books of fairy tales. I saw her one night in a thin white nightgown, seated at her dressing table brushing out that hair. Her head was bent over like a tulip after hard rain, and from the back of her white neck the red hair, catching sparks from a lamp, fell almost to the blue carpet.

I never told Esther about it, but whenever the women whispered, I remembered that scene of sparking hair and lamplight and even then I felt they disapproved of Aunt Celia because anything so beautiful must surely be sinful.

And so the long hot days passed, Michigan summer, with an occasional breeze coming down from Canada to billow white window curtains as we slept. Though I missed my parents and my little brother, too, I didn't really think about them much. In my mind they shrank to manageable proportions so that they and my home and Jackson became to me like an idyllic scene in a glass globe with bits of fake snow swirling all around. I measured my life by Esther's rule, turned my energy to emulating her. Everything about her interested me: the way she tucked fragrant heart-shaped sachets in her underwear drawer, the drops of Tabu she touched to her pulse points before we went walking, the scarlet fingernail polish she applied, leaving white half moons at the cuticle and tips, the way her trim little figure bobbed and bent as she prayed.

On Friday nights and Saturday mornings, Esther

and I went to the synagogue together, walking primly down Linwood Street, outwardly ignoring the boys who swarmed around her, their necks imprisoned in collars and ties, their wiry hair tamed by brilliantine. I fell in and out of love every five minutes. Seated in the balcony between Esther and Aunt Celia, I prayed so fervently and so noisily that Esther poked me in the side and said, "Cut it out. Everyone's looking at you."

The inchoate longing I was beset with, and the knife-blade of emotion that nicked me when I least expected it, I welcomed and even encouraged, bound as they were in my mind to Esther's spell and my desire for spiritual rebirth. The two of us lay in the sun on her back porch reading books from the Duffield branch library. We explored the stores up and down Linwood. In one dusty secondhand shop we found a small leather-bound volume of British poets; Esther bought it for my birthday. I had only to whisper, "Maid of Athens, ere we part, / Give, oh give me back my heart!" and I was reduced to weeping into a little handkerchief I carried now always at the ready. The cantor's wail, quivering past the balcony to the gold-leafed ceilings of Blaine Shul, seemed both an elegy for Jewish suffering through the ages and a validation of my own hunger.

Esther's parents slept in chaste twin beds, as did my Orthodox grandparents, a lamp table between like a bundling board. Esther told me it was a sin for husbands and wives to sleep in double beds because there were times when women were unclean and their husbands were forbidden to go unto them. That's how she put it: "Go unto them." The biblical language and the knowledge of my own parents' wickedly narrow double bed, the one I had thrown tantrums to get into only short years before, tied religion and sex together in a knot I had difficulty picking apart. That and the Yeshiva boys who had begun to put their hands in front of their eyes, palms out like startled starfish, when I passed near them. Esther said they weren't allowed to look at women because it was a sin, and all the while I was trying to purge my own self of sin, I felt vaguely elated at being old enough to be the potential cause of it.

I entered West Intermediate that fall, and Esther went away to school, an Orthodox seminary for girls in Brooklyn. She didn't write, and we lost track of one another for a while. My adolescence progressed normally: enough misery to keep the death wish my usual state, an occasional high to keep me from actually taking the gas-pipe. During one Passover holiday break I spent the night with Esther. My family had moved back to Detroit by then and, surrounded by other Jews, I had finally found a religious balance that didn't have me constantly falling on my face.

That was the year Esther became a blonde. (I sat on the toilet lid and watched her dab on peroxide and ammonia with an old toothbrush.) Without her red hair, she seemed almost a black-and-white version of herself, instead of a study in technicolor. We laughed about the old days, and I called the Rabbi "Uncle David," and even gave him a cool peck on the cheek the way I did my other uncles.

Esther and I lay in bed and bragged about boys, trying to top one another's stories of how far we'd gone with each one. For a little while I thought maybe I had caught up with her at last, but then she told me about some of the crazy girls at her school and how many of them were lesbians. She laughed in an odd, high-pitched way I didn't remember, and grabbed my hand and said, "Lesbian love! Get it?" Oh, I got it, all right. *The Well of Loneliness* had gone through Durfee like the flu that spring, but like most of the books we passed from locker to locker, it raised more questions than it answered.

Esther graduated from the seminary and began attending Wayne University. She smoked cigarettes with other students from the English department and mooned over the popular professors. It wasn't long before word was bruited around the family of one particular boy who was after Esther, not a goy, but in the Rabbi's eyes he might as well have been. My Aunt Ida said that was what they got for letting Esther go to Wayne with all the communists. She knew someone who knew the boy's family. The rumor was they didn't go to shul, even on Yom Kippur. Esther said her friend was an agnostic and told me that she didn't care, and I believed her.

Esther and Ben took to meeting at my house, and once again her life had me in thrall. Ben gave her books to read: *The Sorrows of Werther* and Rilke's *Duino Elegies*. Once Esther showed me something Ben had enclosed in a letter he sent her, a little poem by James Joyce that began, "Lean out of the window, Golden Hair . . ." I envied her that poem as I had once envied her slenderness and the certainty of her prayers. I memorized it, sang it in my bones, a kind of leitmotif, my secular prayer to ward off images of my own fevered and, to me, quite ordinary gropings.

I kept out of the way, discreetly disappearing when Esther and Ben arrived at my house hand in hand, reappearing when Ben left so Esther could lie on my bed and sigh about the hopelessness of it all. She told me they were thinking of running away to Toledo where you could get married without your parents' consent if you were underage. It was all so romantic to me: Romeo and Juliet with a Jewish accent.

One day we headed for Rouge Park in Ben's car, Esther beside him. I remember clearly the old streetcar tracks on Linwood under our wheels, the car lurching from side to side so we slid around on the seats like wrapped packages. "Okay, this is it," Ben said as if he had just thought of it. "We're going to Toledo and get married, and when we come back no one will be able to do anything about it." He turned around and looked straight at me. "You," he said, "will be our witness."

For a moment, it all came crashing in on me: what everyone would say, the cousins, the women. How much of all our lives was wrapped in the cord of their expectations and approval, how much of that cord was wound on the spool of ritual and observance. And I still didn't really know how I felt about it all; I needed a sign from Esther to guide me. We didn't end up in Toledo; Esther got so hysterical that Ben had to turn the car around and take her back to our house.

Later Ben said, "I'm tired of sneaking around like a thief in the night." He told Esther he was going to approach the Rabbi man to man and explain that nothing as reactionary as religion was going to come between him and Esther. He wanted the Rabbi's blessing . . . or else. Esther cried and said all this would kill her father, that he would never forgive her for forsaking her orthodoxy. Ben said, "What century are you people living in anyway?"

One Saturday in October, Ben drove down La Salle and parked directly in front of Esther's house. Hatless and smoking a cigarette, he walked up the winding path to the front door and rang the bell, thereby committing three more sins at once. When he demanded to talk to Esther, smoke trailing out of his mouth, the shocked rabbi ordered him never to see Esther again. That story spread around our family like a kitchen grease fire.

Not long after that, Esther went to live with her sister in New York and we went back to our old lives, a little shaken, as if for a short time we had been mesmerized by flames we had allowed to go unchecked and then, only with difficulty, managed to smother. When I thought about Esther, I spun fanciful tales about renunciation and romance, at once disappointed with her for giving up, and at the same time relieved that she hadn't made my own growing choices more difficult. I imagined that the women finally got to her, that the whispering became too loud for her to ignore.

But now, years later, I wonder about the random nature of choice, the impulsive dart around one corner rather than another, the obscured vision beyond each making the outcome simply one more gamble. Perhaps I have it all wrong. It may be that for Esther being Jewish went far deeper than the shallow surfaces I had been dazzled and fooled by for so long. It may be that in the end she could no more compromise her beliefs than she could change her redheaded nature by bleaching her hair.

I only know that some months later a cousin said she'd heard Esther was engaged to a young rabbi from Queens. I saw her once after she was married. The past stretched between us like a line of flapping wash; we talked about wedding presents and new furniture. And then she went back to New York, and I didn't see her again.

Esther died in childbirth one stone-gray day in winter; she was twenty-one. We brought her home so she could be buried in the cemetery next to her mother. My grandmother, shrunken in her sorrow, skin hanging on her frame like a wrinkled dress, spared me the funeral, for I was married myself by then, and pregnant.

At the Rabbi's house, I wandered from room to empty room, looking for Esther, feeling my childhood crumbling like stale bread. Neighbors and friends had filled the kitchen with food. The table on which we once watched women place their Shabbos chickens was covered with bagels and kaiser rolls, strudel and mandel bread, baskets of fruit so perfect each piece might have been made out of wax. I broke off a cluster of heavy green grapes and carried it up the wide, carpeted stairway to Esther's old room. I could hear the low murmur of voices as the mourners returning from the cemetery rinsed their fingers at an outside faucet before they entered the house.

In front of Esther's vanity, I sat on a bench and stared into the shrouded mirror. With a tiny pair of gold scissors she once used to trim her nails, I cut a slash in the collar of my dress, and then I ate the green grapes slowly, one by one. When I finished, I closed my eyes and said a made-up prayer for Esther. "Lean out of the window," I whispered, tasting the sweet flesh of green grapes. "Lean out of the window, Golden Hair."

I STILL REMEMBER SUMMER'S end in Michigan, when leaves begin to let go of their green and autumn evenings may occasionally reveal the bared and glittering teeth of winter. Then comes time again for lingering at the table after cozy suppers and for long-neglected school books open under lamplight's golden pools.

Of course we couldn't confess to a surfeit of summer, but by Labor Day most of us children were ready to shuck off shorts and sandals, eager to view in the shoe store's X-ray machine room for toes to grow in brand new lace-up shoes.

And we were confident she would be waiting, Miss This or Mrs. That, our teacher whose existence outside of school had no more reality for us than did the flesh under the dark dresses she invariably wore. We would have been shocked to encounter her away from the classroom, would have ducked our heads in embarrassment to witness anything so unseemly as a schoolteacher in a dimestore or at a picture show.

Like our mother who pushed us out the door in the morning and hung in a state of suspended animation until our safe return, our schoolteacher was defined by the space she occupied. So, tanned, mosquito-bitten, fattened up on homegrown sweet corn and tomatoes, we marched back to school to pierce the briar hedge and rouse her from her summer slumber.

Another fall is almost here. The acrid smell of chalk dust will soon mingle with the smoke of burning leaves. Now I am a grown-up and a schoolteacher myself. Crazily, I find some of what I believed so long ago is true. A part of me sleeps each summer and waits in limbo until that morning early in September when the first student walks into my classroom and by her presence brings me fully back to life again.

I WAS SPENDING THE NIGHT, I remember, curled up spoon-fashion in a bed next to my cousin in the finished attic of my aunt and uncle's house in Detroit. My own family was home in Jackson a couple of hours away. Perhaps I was awake missing my parents the way kids do; perhaps the unfamiliar city night-sounds had aroused me. Far, far off, mingled with streetcar clang and the occasional rattle of a passing auto, I heard the voice of a newsboy hawking papers. Gradually, as he neared, the words cut through the steamy night air and engraved themselves forever on my memory. "Extra! Extra!" the boy shouted. "Will Rogers and Wiley Post crash in waters off Alaska!"

I was only five years old on that torrid August night in 1935, but I knew, with the unerring antennae children have, that the part of the world I was conscious of had suffered a grievous loss. That is my first recollection of public tragedy and grief; sadly, it has not been my last.

In the small independent school where I teach English, word of the space shuttle *Challenger*'s fate spread from classroom to classroom late one morning in January. By lunchtime, many students were clustered in front of TVs in the computer room, looking for the visual confirmation they have grown up with and come to expect. At normal speed and in slow motion, again and again, they watched a nation's dream dissolve in a spectacular bloom of flame.

When Will Rogers died, I doubt that anyone thought to discuss with me my feelings of loss or anxiety. My immigrant parents, forced into early adulthood by circumstance, were determined their own children would have long, untarnished golden years of growing up. So when children were around, in our family as in many others of the time, people would simply have acted as if that airplane crash had never happened.

Still, we had avenues for grief. The old rituals ensured that death, never diminished, took its natural place in the continuum of human existence. In accordance with Jewish custom, we sat shivah for our dead, rent our clothing, removed our shoes and, seated on low mourner's benches, were comforted with cakes and fruit and moments to share memories of those we'd lost.

It's no longer the fashion to shield children from the sadness of life. We could hardly do it if we wanted to—short of locking them away like Sleeping Beauty or Rapunzel. Certainly it's no coincidence that the age of television and instant communication coincides with a new candor in relationships, encouraging children to express all their emotions, not just the positive ones. "Getting in touch with our feelings" has become a cliché, but ironically, the extended family and close-knit community structures that helped us deal with those feelings in the past have now shrunk to vestigial tails. "It's okay to cry," we say as we blockade the old roads by which we might have traveled our sorrow.

I wonder, for example, how many schoolchildren went home to empty houses the day the *Challenger* went down. If my own seventh graders are typical, they unlocked the front door, turned on the nearest TV set, and until one or both parents came home, they confronted the exploding shuttle over and over again—alone.

I've often thought about the enormous responsibility parents have passed on to us teachers. The average family with school-age children spends four or five waking hours under the same roof. Every day, teachers are in charge of those kids for seven to nine hours a day. We discipline them, counsel them, offer them a value system (consciously or not), and when a monstrous tragedy like the *Challenger* explosion invades their lives, we help them put it in perspective.

No sooner had the *Challenger* met its end than experts were exhorting us to allow our children to grieve. Once again, as when the film *The Day After* was shown, schools were asked to supply the sense of community we seem to be losing. For both teachers and students, the death of teacher Christa McAuliffe made the tragedy more personal, and so more painful. Thus, at least in the case of the *Challenger*, school was a poetically appropriate place to come together with our sadness.

At my school, we learn a lot about reading and writing in our English class. We do vocabulary drills and spelling, and practice writing clear paragraphs—the usual fare for seventh grade. But our classroom is also the setting for general discussion. I want my students to be able to listen to one another as well as offer opinions. Language is paramount, and we use it to inform, persuade, and delight.

So I had no qualms about allowing my students to sit shivah, symbolically, in their English class. But I worried that I might not be able to orchestrate the hour sensitively enough, that my students might leave the room without having been helped to understand that it is human to mourn and that the language of community can take the edge off deepest grief.

When my students were finally in their seats the day after the *Challenger*'s ill-fated launch, I studied them a moment before I began. Seventh graders are marvelous.

They enter school in September still children; the boys punch each other a lot, and the girls, just a step ahead, eye them with obvious distaste. Things are different after Christmas, a happening as inevitable as sunrise. The boys' baby fat begins to melt; their legs between hip and knee grow as if on yeast. Now the first traces of pairing off begin, and suddenly a group has formed where only weeks earlier two armed camps existed side by side. For all their squabbling and bickering, these kids before me that morning were a family at last, and it was as a family that I addressed them.

I began by reading the president's speech aloud. Although many of my students had heard it the night before, I felt its simple expression of mourning, coupled with hope for the future, might set the tone for the discussion that would follow. Afterward, we talked about our reactions to what had happened, where we were when we first heard the news, and what information we had to explain the accident.

And then, because only human beings can make art out of tragedy, I invited my students to write about their feelings; I wanted them to put on paper an event that would be part of their memories as long as they lived (the way the newsboy shouting "Extra!" was for me).

As if he had read my thoughts, one child wrote, "Seven lives taken in a matter of seconds, feelings of joy dispersing into depression and sadness. I did not know the people, knew only one name, yet I was crushed, shocked and saddened by this event that will affect me the rest of my life."

"I don't know why," wrote one of my girls, "but when someone dies, the tears of sadness don't come first. It's guilt: guilt for this or guilt for that. Those kids [the children of the crew] must have thought right off, 'And I never told her this or showed him that.'"

But perhaps the most telling words of all came from the boy who wrote, "I hope the kids of the astronauts take the news well, and I hope the press leaves them alone. But most of all, I feel for the schoolchildren who lost their teacher and saw her die live on TV."

"*Die live.*" I shook my head in wonder. It took a twelve-year-old child to name the horror in two small words. Die live. Oh, my dear, that's it. We live on fast-forward with no time to cushion our encounters.

When the bell rang my students filed out quietly, for a change. I sat at my desk, unwilling to surrender the moment. I didn't know if the *kids* felt any better, but their words had surely comforted *me*. A teacher will yet go up in space, I thought, but for the moment I feel, with Robert Frost, that "*Earth's the right place for love: / I don't know where it's likely to go better.*"

It isn't much of a farmhouse—white-painted stucco over yellow pine logs with ceilings so low my six-foot-plus son-in-law is an endangered species every time he visits. But it's in the foothills of Virginia's Blue Ridge, just about two hours from our home in Washington, DC, and we've been spending weekends there for years.

Last year my husband and I did some cosmetic surgery on the place—a bit of barn siding and Sheetrock to shore up the ceilings and interior walls, some so crooked we might have been living in a Dali dreamscape. When our small downstairs bedroom was finished, we painted the paneling white. I spread a white quilt on the four-poster bed and hung on one wall another quilt I had bargained for at a local flea market.

This quilt had been made in the twenties, or so I guessed from the soft greens, lavenders, pinks, and blues of the tiny triangles pieced in intersecting chains all across the bleached white background. I wondered sometimes about its maker. I imagined her, a mother like myself, bent over the steadily evolving beauty she was creating from the remnants of her life. Surely it was a sublime economy that made a work of art out of what might otherwise have been discarded.

I loved the completed room. Unlike so much of my life, it was pure and uncluttered. The very absence of color, except for the design of the quilt on the wall, seemed to render it one of the most perfect spaces I had ever seen. I resented anything which disturbed that perfection, even my husband's shoes on the floor or a pair of jeans slung over the single chair.

At home in the city, not long after the renovations were finished, I received a frantic phone call: three volunteer fire companies were fighting flames that had started inside the yellow pine walls of the refurbished bedroom. Once again I learned how fragile perfection is. All I could think of was that no insurance policy, no matter how inclusive, could ever replace the nameless woman's quilt with its softly blazing triangles.

Still, I had no control over the situation. Nothing I could do would affect the outcome. I phoned my husband and told him the news. Then, in the way of women, I scoured pots and swept floors, awaiting further word. And while feverishly scrubbing and cleaning, I remembered something my mother used to tell me.

paid off debts, rebuilding financial security dollar by dollar. One happy day, a delivery van replaced our old lumpy davenport and sagging easy chair with spindly-legged burled maple and fruitwood furniture. One piece especially captured my imagination: a glass-shelved and velvet-lined curio cabinet that stood on curved legs as delicate as a thoroughbred's.

Inside the cabinet, my mother kept a collection of small English bone china cups, each gold-rimmed and banded in a different jewel-like color. Perhaps to her the tiny cups symbolized an end to want and economic insecurity; I know she loved them. She made a ceremony of washing them each week, using a heavy Turkish towel to cushion the translucent china in the porcelain sink.

Clara, who helped my mother, was gingerly dusting the curio cabinet with a feather duster one afternoon when she knocked over a cup and broke off its handle. I had been reading nearby and saw her crying as she carried the two fragments of china to my mother. I thought Clara wept for the pretty cup. I didn't know then that she feared she might be fired; hard times were still more than a memory for many in those days.

My mother blanched when she realized what lay in Clara's hands. But after a few moments she said, "In our family we call this kind of accident a *kapore*." She reached out and took the pieces, cradling them in her palm. "You see, the broken cup takes the place of harm that might have come to one of us. Don't cry, Clara," she said, "everything can be replaced except a human life."

My mother died not many years after that. The collection of dainty cups came to me, and I gave them a place of honor in my first home. I think I loved them even more than my mother had; their beauty was bound up with her memory. They sat on a small wooden shelf in my bedroom—eleven perfect cups and one with a mended handle. I, too, washed them as my mother had, cushioning the kitchen sink with a folded bath towel. I allowed no one to touch the cups but me. Sometimes I would take them down, one by one, to show to my little daughter. I told her that the tiny cups with their brilliant bands of color would someday belong to her.

One winter morning while I worked in another part of the house, my daughter climbed on a chair to reach the cups. She must have lost her balance; by the time I heard the crash, she lay on the floor, the shelf on top of her. Of the cups, only a profusion of bright colored shards remained.

Heart pounding, I snatched up my howling child and frantically felt her head for bumps. I peered into her streaming eyes. Had she been cut or even blinded by flying glass? When I determined that she wasn't really hurt, I took her on my lap. As in a dream, my mother's words came back to me. "Those were only china cups," I crooned, rocking my daughter back and forth. "They can be replaced. Only you, my precious, cannot be replaced . . ."

MY HUSBAND AND I DROVE TO THE FARM THE DAY AFTER THE fire, grateful to find much of the house still standing. In the dimly lit shambles of that once-perfect bedroom, I felt my way through splintered wood and broken glass until my fingers touched a sodden bundle of cloth. Hugging the quilt to my breast, I carried it into the sunshine and spread it on the grass. Half-covered in soot and reeking of the fire that had almost consumed it, a corner of the quilt survived, its luminous triangles still triumphantly marching.

As we go about the tedious task of rebuilding, I think often of the nameless woman patiently piecing scraps of pink and blue and green, a vision of perfection spurring her needle. Her lesson is that beauty and wholeness can be created from broken pieces. But broken pieces—scraps of fabric, shards of china, the ruins of a farmhouse—remind me of an even more important lesson.

I tell myself the quilt I cherished so is the *kapore*, the object that took the place of harm that might otherwise have come to one of us. My mother's lesson is the most significant of all, for no material thing, no matter how beloved, can ever have the value of a human life.

I CUT MY HORTICULTURAL TEETH, so to speak, on a victory garden I grew as a child in the backyard of our Michigan home during World War II. I remember simply that things grew with a Jack-and-the-beanstalk speed and certainty. A Flit gun and citronella candles kept winged predators at bay; we were too citified for four-legged pests. Only my grandfather, poking his cane among the cool green leaves in search of young cucumbers, disturbed the tranquility of my contribution to the war effort.

Years later, transplanted to Washington, my husband and I bought some land in rural Virginia and, spurred by rising food costs, fear of pesticides, and memories of past gardening glories, I convinced him to join me in trying farming once more.

The first spring we plowed and planted under the disdainful eyes of the locals, who didn't even bother to hide their amusement behind a turned-out palm. The hay mulch method, a boon to weekend gardeners, must have provided them with some real thigh-smackers. They knew how many weed seeds slept in that hay, awaiting resurrection by sun and water.

Early seedlings pushed their way though earth crumbs in April, and by the first of May feathery carrot tops, graceful pea plants, and tender lettuce made the taut strings marking rows unnecessary. Flushed with success, we bought out Clark's Hardware on Saturday, filled the station wagon with flats of broccoli, brussels sprouts, cauliflower, and cabbage. Late that afternoon, barely able to walk after having been on my knees all day, I savored my reward: brave rows of sturdy plants standing up to salute the sun. We drank a lot of beer that night, and my dreams danced with baskets of broccoli, carloads of cabbage.

Early the next morning I ran to the garden. There was only one problem—overnight it had all but disappeared. Tasting gall, I surveyed the ruin: the rows of lettuce shaved as if by some gargantuan razor, carrot tops gone, my peas reduced to a few pathetic tendrils, and my new plants— the product of all that labor—leafless. They looked like green miniatures of the mercilessly pruned plane trees that line the streets of European cities in the spring.

Of course I knew what the trouble was. Hadn't I read every gardening book known to man? My confident diagnosis was cutworms, and I would foil them or risk displacing a disc doing it. Undaunted, I went back to the hardware store and bought another wagonload of plants. This time I protected each plant with a paper collar or an empty tin can, top and bottom removed.

The next morning, when the tin cans were kicked over, the paper collars thrust aside and the plants gone again, I realized I was dealing either with an unspeakably strong mutation of a cutworm, or, worse yet, what the locals grimly, and with much satisfaction assured me was a GROUNDHOG. The locals were right, of course—they always are—and ever since, we and the groundhog have been locked in a deadly struggle for possession of the garden.

Most of the time, the groundhog wins paws down. Understand, we are peaceful people, for gun control, against the National Rifle Association, and yet, put a rifle in my hands today, point it in the right direction, and I would blow a groundhog to kingdom come without a moral quiver. We started out peacefully enough, planting double rows of everything, half for the groundhog, half for us. I think at that point the groundhog brought in a few friends from nearby farms. The job was too big for him to accomplish alone.

We do not lack for sympathetic ears now. It's no longer City Slicker versus Pea Picker, and war stories abound. United by a common enemy, we stand on the loading platform of the Culpeper Farmers' Cooperative, cackling as someone named Jenkins or Kilby or Fincham heaves fertilizer sacks and reminisces about the time he got a groundhog by exploding a gallon jug of gasoline in its hole with a rifle shell.

We have our own stories to tell. We have skulked around the groundhog's hole after dusk and set off smoke bombs (say "bums" in Culpeper) until we're sure we have done irreparable harm to our own lungs. The groundhog, like the boll weevil, "takes it like a man." One day we stopped up all the other holes we could find and backed our car up to the "main entrance." We pumped in auto exhaust and then closed the hole with a boulder. The next day the groundhog ate cucumber vines to teach us a lesson. Groundhogs don't even *like* cucumber vines.

Macbeth's witches could have concocted no more noxious brews than those we have mixed to convince the groundhog he would be happier elsewhere. Mixtures of ammonia and creosote, the contents of a chemical toilet, enough mothballs to protect a woolen mill—nothing "phrases him," as a neighbor puts it. We have pounded logs into the holes with the zeal of one pounding a stake through the heart of a vampire, and the groundhog just digs out around them. An electric fence? He crawls under. A trap? Why does he need to bother with bait when there's a whole world of garden out there for him to enjoy?

In a crazy sense, we have come to feel a kind of kinship with the groundhog, the way hostages are said to grow sympathetic toward their captors. We see him as a Beatrix Potter figure; imagine him bespectacled, down there reading the *Groundhog Gazette*, his gas mask at the ready, slung over the arm of his Morris chair. The year we planted lettuce seed brought back from France, we could visualize him leafing through Julia Child, hunting for a recipe for salade Niçoise.

This year we have tried something different. In the middle of our garden stands a figure in a blue wash dress and a faded straw hat that has "Virginia" embroidered on it. From her wooden arms dangle aluminum pie plates that clash in the wind and small cowbells that occasionally tinkle. We don't have much hope for it. We can see the old groundhog, paws folded over the potbelly he owes to us, telling his wife, "The Moskowitzes must really be desperate; that's the oldest one in the book!"

Sooner or later most fami-
lies, and communities as well, forge their own shared
sense of what they consider appropriate ways to live.
From politics to perfume, philosophy to food, a standard
is set by which outsiders are measured (and usually found
wanting). Back home in Detroit, where I come from, I
learned early to recognize the slightly disdainful curl of
the lip that preceded any sentence that began "By us,"
for whatever followed was certain to have inherent in it
a disparaging comparison to the way others felt or did
things. "By us" implied a comfortable certainty about the
way life was to be conducted.

While that kind of certainty can provide security for a
child growing up, the necessary exploration that maturity
makes almost inevitable can then become a bit complicated. It isn't easy to justify blazing a new trail when the
old one is practically a four-lane highway. One solution
is to put some physical space between yourself and the
people you have grown up with. Then you can continue

to hold fast to the values and customs with which you are comfortable, while you do some minor experimentation in peace.

In 1962, my husband and I moved ourselves and four children to Washington, DC. Leaving our extended family in the treeless suburbs outside Detroit to which they had migrated by then, we bought a sprawling Victorian home in town and proceeded to furnish the warren of rooms with a motley collection of early Goodwill and late thrift shop. We thought the place looked pretty good until my Uncle Phil, the developer, came to visit us from Michigan. He looked around at the leaded glass falling from its frames, at the ancient bathtubs stolidly resting on ball and claw. He inspected the cramped little closets and the Medusa's heads of extension cords bristling from the woefully scarce electrical outlets.

"Faygie," he said delicately, staring up at a large crack in the plaster, "what did you have to pay here for such a house?" I saw the lip begin to curl. Never mind that houses in our neighborhood were in such demand that real estate agents circled like vultures when they heard a resident was ailing. Never mind that "fashionable Cleveland Park" was the frequent subject of the *Post* Sunday supplements. Forget that half the kids of what we came to know as "Camelot" played scrub ball in the empty lot next door. "By us," my uncle said, washing his hands of the whole affair, "you couldn't get a mortgage on a place like this."

It didn't get better. Later that year, one of my cousins decided to make a trip to Washington. I invited her "for coffee," a form of entertainment "by us" that involves schmoozing endlessly around a table laden with a week's worth of groceries: sliced cheeses and bagels, rich coffee cakes, kuchen, seven-layer cakes, Napoleons. We ourselves didn't eat that way any longer, of course, but I wasn't taking any chances with curled lips and comparisons. For days before the visit I readied the house, taking down dusty curtains, polishing the furniture, scrubbing the bathroom tile. With only minutes to spare, I put the finishing gloss on the hardwood floors that were my special pride, acres of gleaming boards with an oriental rug scattered here and there for jeweled accent.

"I think everything went off really well," I told my husband when we were finally in bed that night. "They seemed to like the house, and nobody could complain that we didn't have enough food. We're going to be eating it the rest of the month." It was two weeks before the reverberations reached me from back home, and in a way I asked for it. "How did Sally like the house?" I casually asked my Aunt Bessie on long distance one afternoon. The pause that followed should have alerted me. Aunt Bessie does not consider "outspoken" a pejorative word. "I hate to tell you this, . . ." she began at last, and my heart sank. "To tell you the truth," she went on, "Sally asked me if Jack was making a living." "What kind of question is that?" I asked hotly. "What's the problem, I didn't feed her enough?" "It's not that," Aunt Bessie said, "it's your floors." "What's wrong with my floors? They're gorgeous!" "Floors are floors," said my aunt. "You know how it is. By us they go for wall-to-wall."

Actually, we were too busy adjusting to our surroundings to pay much attention to the opinion of folks back home. By the time my old friend Sylvia came down for one of the peace marches, I felt secure enough about my new way of living to do a little showing off. We had been invited to a dinner party where the host was famous for his versions of French haute cuisine. I wangled an invitation for Sylvia and boasted just a little to her about previous gourmet feasts we had enjoyed in that same house. Sylvia looked a little doubtful, and I wasn't so long from home that I didn't remember that in the sixties exotic food "by us" was pizza and egg foo yong. "Don't worry," I said patronizingly, "I had to get used to some of the cooking around here myself."

The night of the dinner party, our neighbors outdid themselves: pâté, cassoulet, soufflé—everything rhymed. I kept glancing over to where Sylvia sat toying with her food, dazzled, I was sure, by the elegantly appointed table and the sparkling conversation by some of Washington's great and near-great. She'll have plenty to say when she gets home, I thought smugly. Actually, I was right. She did have plenty to say. I was simply wrong about what she said.

When the translucent dessert plates were cleared away (Minton, I had noted with satisfaction earlier, after surreptitiously peeking under the rim), demitasse was served. I looked over at Sylvia again, just as she was reaching for the tiny glass-lined silver dish in front of her. Helplessly I watched her stir two heaping spoonfuls of salt into her coffee.

"Shall we take our cups into the living room?" asked our hostess. In the slight crush that ensued, I lost any chance to subtly warn Sylvia of her mistake. Too late, I stared fascinated as she took a sip from her cup, balancing the saucer carefully on her lap. I'll say this much: to her credit, she didn't miss a beat. Sip after delicate sip, she downed that demitasse.

We walked home from the party after midnight, my husband, Sylvia, and I, the women's heels clacking on the quiet sidewalks. Sylvia seemed lost in thought. While my husband fumbled at the lock of our front door, she plucked at my shoulder. I remember that even in the light of the leaf-shrouded street lamp, I could see the curl of her lip. "Okay," she said, "so we aren't so sophisticated back home, and we don't throw fancy dinner parties and we don't all cook gourmet, but I'll tell you one thing— at least by us we know how to make a decent cup of coffee!" With that she turned and marched triumphantly up the stairs.

My son Seth commiserated with me. "In this family," he said, pushing his chair back from the table, "food is the recreational drug of choice." We were having a little snack and talking about my nephew's upcoming wedding in Michigan. No one knows better than recovering foodaholics like us what millstones these ceremonial milestones can be. "I'm plenty worried about backsliding," I told Seth. "The way I see it, every social event back there becomes a perverse game of 'chicken.' The hosts try to lay out an ever more tempting spread, while half the guests who walk in have just gone on a diet and are trying to see how close they can get to the table without eating anything."

As my trip back home for the wedding approached, I found myself daydreaming about the succulent chicken feet and the chewy unborn eggs my mother used to fish out of the chicken soup for me just before the Sabbath. I remembered the calf's feet that my grandmother cooked down to a sticky brown gravy for sopping with hunks of challah, and so tender the meat fell off the bones. I thought of my widowed grandfather when he had nearly reached the century mark, still smacking his lips over a little pot of "fish potatoes" he had prepared for himself: sautéed onions and sliced potatoes, cooked in milk and black with pepper. Down the shadowy tunnels of memory I saw myself a child again, legs dangling from my chair, an overflowing bowl in front of me and my mother in her flowered housedress whispering, "*Ess, ess, mein kind.*"

So I was on guard the moment I hit the outskirts of the Detroit suburbs where everyone lives now in sprawling subdivisions named Country Club Estates and Hunt Country Villas, each sub attached to a satellite shopping mall supporting what appears to be one restaurant for every two families. My brother Hymie picked me up at the airport and took me to lunch at Denny's, along with his children and grandchildren. I read the six-page menu from cover to cover, refusing to be tempted by the siren call of oil-slicked fries or mayonnaise-girdled BLTs or the crispy corn dogs the kids seemed to favor. Instead I opted for a short stack of buttermilk pancakes, congratulating myself on the "short" and carefully scraping away the melting butter ball that skated on top when my order arrived. A meal at a time, I kept telling myself, breathing slowly and deeply. Maybe I'd come back to Fat City, but

I hadn't spent the last twenty-five years in less-is-more, pressure-cooker Washington without learning some lessons in casting off the food chain.

That evening I took Hy and my sister-in-law, Barb, out to dinner to catch up on family gossip. One thing I might as well admit from the start: the restaurant was my choice. Now I know as well as the next guy that one way to break old habits is to avoid the situations that foster them, so you could say I walked into the Stage Deli with my eyes (and my mouth) wide open. All the butter scraping I did at Denny's was an empty gesture, for the moment I caught the garlicky salt scent of the Stage, I fell off the wagon. "Let's start with an order of old dills," I told my brother, my fingers already trembling as I turned the glossy oversized pages of the menu. Barb, who had gone back to Weight Watchers as soon as her son's engagement was announced, had no trouble deciding on the Mark Beltaire: a plate of Spartan greens and white meat turkey, with the salad dressing on the side. Hy, who has other fish to fry, asked for a chopped liver plate with an order of bread which arrived in a basket: warm, chewy rye bread you can get your teeth into, and believe me I did, while I munched juicy pickles and waited for my sandwich and diet cherry cola.

What can I tell you about my choice of sandwich except that despite a pathological fear of flying, I once hitched a ride home to Michigan on a small private plane because I was suffering from severe Dinty Moore deprivation. The four-inch layer of warm corned beef brisket melting in the mouth, the lettuce, tomato, Russian dressing, and toasted white bread combine to form a sandwich that is for Jews the moral equivalent of the forbidden BLT. No way to fool myself; after that first bite I was lost.

For warm-ups the next day, Saturday morning, I ate whatever my hotel offered in the way of a complimentary breakfast—orange juice, corn flakes, Danish, and coffee. I needed my strength, I told myself, fighting off an incipient anxiety attack. At 9:30 I was due at the synagogue for a long service during which our nephew would be called to the altar in a traditional prenuptial ceremony. Remembering the endless Shabbos mornings of my childhood, I grabbed another pastry and ate it on the way out of the hotel.

At the Orthodox synagogue I took my place, meekly enough, behind the screen which divided the men from the women. Yes, I groused about a religion that makes second-class citizens of fifty percent of its members, but my plate was already too full for serious protests; I was so far gone that my mouth actually watered at the hard candies given out toward the end of the service. These had been placed in plastic baggies and reserved for that moment in the ceremony when the women stand at the partition and pelt the groom with sugar to ensure a sweet life. I primly buried myself in my prayer book, all the while berating myself for not having brought along an extra Danish from breakfast; I could have downed it in the ladies' room.

After the service we all adjourned to the social hall, where a long table had been set up for a Grand Kiddush to which the entire congregation had been invited. This was no simple kiddush like those I remembered from childhood, with whiskey neat in little shot glasses and Manischewitz wine and pickled herring. In those days, I had had sense enough to stay out of the line of fire, considering myself no match for the old guys who could belly up to the refreshments with lethal elbows and practiced hips. By the time they had had their fill, the table was a wasteland of empty plates and challah crumbs.

Today the guests were treated to gefilte fish and fiery horseradish, chopped liver, herring, pickles, hummus, pita bread, olives, cantaloupe, honeydew, watermelon, cakes, and cookies. Astonishingly, the old men were there, too, as if they had been lying in cold storage in their rusty gabardines, waiting all this time for the Grand Kiddush to revive them. I knew I was still a tyro in the midst of these experienced trenchermen; I had no more stomach for mixing it up with them on this day that I had years before. Besides, my brother had told me that this kiddush featured a *cholent*, and I was eager to renew acquaintances with a dish that had grown in my memory to emblematic proportions.

I should have been alerted when the bride's mother called it "chunt." Any good Litvak knows it's pronounced "cho-lent," and the dish served at our paper-clad trestle tables bore little resemblance to my family's version except that, like ours, it had clearly been subjected to the indignity of over twenty hours in the oven. Still, the beauty of *cholent* is that it can be prepared and set to bake well before sundown on Friday night, when the lighting of fires is proscribed. All through the evening and night and even during the Sabbath service, the ingredients grow ever more anonymous until they completely lose their identity in a tender mélange whose scent can be discerned halfway home from the synagogue.

This "chunt" was made of barley, navy beans, and potatoes and the usual brisket or flank meat that tends to fall apart and mysteriously disappear sometime during the latter half of the cooking. I have never eaten *cholent* without some defensive housewife swearing that she had put a fortune of meat in it and couldn't understand where it had gone. There was much reminiscing among the cousins at our table about the way our Bobbe had made *cholent* with potatoes and lima beans, a version we preferred. We all agreed, however, that the meat problem clearly crossed *stetl* lines because no one remembered anyone but Zayde getting any, and *cholent* or "chunt," today was no exception. In the spirit of fellowship, I put aside my personal nostalgia and managed two helpings.

After the kiddush, some of us went to Cranbrook to see the Miles statues. I was desperate to walk off the "chunt" before the potatoes settled, whole, in the saddlebags on my thighs, a tendency for which the dish is famous. By three o'clock my brother Reuben, a notorious coward who, like me, had not had the guts to mix it up at the buffet table, was hungry. We headed for the Ram's Horn and another menu as big as the Ritz. There we discovered that not only could we order the hot fudge ice cream cake, but Weight Watcher's tofutti if that was our pleasure. My brother had a Char Burger, my sister-in-law the soft ice cream, while I, simply for the challenge, tossed back a whipped-cream-bedecked wedge of banana cream pie so tall it defied gravity.

By then it was time to go to Hy and Barb's for the out-of-towner's dinner, and there was no stopping me; I was ready to put on the lampshade (and the feedbag), too. Barb, who had decided "not to fuss" had settled for "ordering in a tray." I did my best to accommodate her, picking at the chewy Detroit bagels, cream cheese, lox, pickled herring, smoked sable and chubs, sliced muenster and swiss cheese, lokshen kugel, blintz soufflé, clusters of grapes and tiny balls of watermelon, cantaloupe, and honeydew, all washed down with the ubiquitous diet soda. Reuben tells me I had both the black forest cake and the kiwi torte, but I'm ashamed to admit I don't remember a thing after the second helping of kugel.

Sunday morning brunch at the home of old friends passed in a blur. I seem to recall more bagels, onion rolls, smoked salmon, creamed herring, and French coffee that could have pierced a pea-soup fog even thicker than the one in which I was enveloped. Perhaps it was the coffee that awakened me long enough to try the all-butter streusel-topped coffee cake and its companion, one filled with a sweet burden of cream cheese gently laced with cinnamon.

Back at the hotel where my husband had now joined me, I stared at the woman in the mirror, who returned my scrutiny reproachfully. She looked bloated, dissolute, ashamed. The main bout was coming up, and she'd never pass the weigh-in. It was too late for good intentions or liposuction; I clutched at my only recourse, my mantra: "A meal at a time, a meal at a time."

And all during the cocktail hour after the wedding ceremony, I repeated it again, "A meal at a time," as I passed up the chicken tenders, the Swedish meatballs, the kreplach, the egg rolls, the fried mushrooms. When the waitress passed the tray of kosher pigs-in-blankets under my nose for the third time, I broke out in a cold sweat. Just one, I told myself. After all it's a wedding. You don't want to be a party pooper. What harm can one little . . . I popped the morsel in my mouth, bit through the flaky crust to the chewy spicy hot dog, nonchalantly flipped the toothpick back on the tray, and went under for the last time.

There was no controlling me at the dinner that followed. I would have eaten the tall centerpiece of white carnations and glads if there hadn't already been a relish tray to occupy me. I munched olives and carrot sticks and celery stalks, impatient for the blessing to be said so I could devour the tiny braided challah at my place. I hardly noticed the other guests at our table for eight, so intent was I on slurping the thick mushroom barley soup the waiters ladled into each of our bowls. I picked at my green salad and impatiently waved away the lemon sorbet that followed, too hardcore to care for anything but the hard stuff.

The waiters staggered in under trays laden with steaming covered plates. As is usual at affairs like these, someone at the table sighed over her portion of a full half chicken. "It's such a waste," she said. "Who can eat so much?" I knew who, but I wasn't telling. Besides, I also knew that if a mere quarter chicken had been served, people would have immediately begun speculating about the health of the bride's father's business. "The Oldsmobile syndrome," my cousin Bob calls it, "putting up a good front." Speaking of fronts, I had given up on mine as I scarfed the chicken, mixed vegetables, crumb-topped mashed potatoes, all the while enviously regarding my husband's plate, speculating whether he was going to finish his slice of kishke, a luscious but lethal mixture of flour, fat, carrots, onions, and spices, stuffed into a casing and baked to a fare-thee-well.

By the time I came to, I realized that the wedding guests were already lining up for the "sweet table," a mile-long affair centered by a cascading cornucopia of whole fruit: plums, tangerines, plump bunches of grapes, wedges of watermelon, and a migrant worker's daily quota of fresh strawberries. On either side of the fruit, chocolate, hazelnut, and strawberry tortes vied for center stage with lemon and kiwi and blueberry tarts. Cauldrons of non-dairy "whipped cream" waited to be slathered on top of whatever suited anyone's fancy, while mounds of strudel, rugelach, chocolate chip cookies, and brownies modestly put themselves forth.

I made a weak pass at the fruit for propriety's sake, and then parked myself in front of the halvah molded into the size and shape of a cinder block. There was no stopping me. I stood wolfing the sesame and sugar confection while cousins and aunts politely pumped me about my children and my grandchild, all of whom I would have sold into slavery for one more slice of the Middle East's contribution to my total debauchery. In fact the only thought in my head was a persistent worry that my husband might want to leave before the cake-cutting ceremony.

I'm back in Washington now, my lost weekend only a guilty memory. I have considered Betty Ford and Hazeldon, but in the end decided I could handle going cold turkey on carrot sticks by myself. Some days are harder than others, and then I remember my mantra: "A meal at a time." It doesn't help much.

W E JEWS KNOW THERE IS NO such thing as a Jewish paranoiac because, as the old joke goes, everything we worry about is true. I think of that sometimes when I remember the Passover of the Blood Accusation at my father's house sometime back in the fifties. The first seder fell on a Friday night that year, for I recall we were well into the additional Sabbath prayers when we first noticed something unusual was happening.

There were ten of us gathered in the pine-paneled "rec room" that my father, a carpenter, had created in the basement. Like Frank Lloyd Wright, Daddy insisted on designing his own furnishings; he was especially proud of the wet bar covered in red leatherette and punctuated by the design of a bubbling cocktail glass picked out in brass nailheads. Now, leaning on two down pillows in an overstuffed chair, reclining as the festive nature of Passover decrees, my father looked with satisfaction around the damask-clad ping-pong table, pressed into service for the holiday.

Together we read the service from our Haggadahs, drank wine at the appropriate times, and dipped greens and bitter herbs in little saucers of salt water. As Jews have done for centuries in diverse settings all over the world, we were once again experiencing Exodus as though it were happening at that very moment.

After a while, we came to that point many people reach in the course of a seder, when the participants split into two factions: the conservatives and the liberals. The conservatives, of course, insist on reading every word in the Haggadah and love to go off into long Talmudic tangents about each line, while the liberals want to streamline the entire affair and get to the food. Concentration is difficult sometimes as the debate and the service, with its intermittent glosses, wear on, and visions of matzo balls begin dancing in the head.

My little brother was just starting to slip down in the chair from which he would shortly disappear under the table, when I realized some foreign odor was vying with the familiar aroma of roasting chicken and cinnamon-kissed carrot pudding: the acrid smell of something burning. Just above our heads in the low-ceilinged room, plumes of smoke hugged the acoustical tile.

Now normal people, it seems to me, follow a predictable course here. You smell smoke, you call the fire department and head for the nearest exit. But my father, born in czarist Russia where paranoia was endemic, leaned against his pillows as we began milling about, knocking over wine glasses, spilling matzo crumbs from our laps onto the floor. "Just a second," he said. "Take it easy." I'm sure he assumed that the fire, if it was indeed a fire, was about to be blamed on him. He didn't want any firemen poking about his house making accusations.

"Daddy," I said, between gritted teeth, "would you get OUT of here?" Born and raised in America, I had grown up in the Officer Friendly generation, so I had little sympathy for my father's fear of anything in brass buttons. "Everybody leave," I yelled officiously. "I'll call the fire department." In moments, it appeared, sirens were at our front door, and rubber-slickered firemen, axes poised, sprang from every side of the glistening fire trucks.

By this time we were all in the front yard, where my father gave me a look that could have easily become the eleventh plague. "Boyehs," he said feebly, turning toward the firemen, "the door is open. Don't chop down a good birch door." (If there was anything my father had respect for it was wood.)

"There's your problem," shouted the chief, ignoring my father. He pointed to the second story, the flat where Tante Leah lived. Sirens are irresistible. In moments our tree-lined street had rapidly filled with women in their holiday best, standing around, arms folded under their bosoms. At their sides stood little girls in hair ribbons and party dresses. Men and boys in yarmulkes, the men in suits, the boys in two-tone leisure jackets and clip-on bow ties, were everywhere. We all looked up to where the chief was pointing. Bright flames danced a lively *kazachka* in Tante Leah's picture window.

"Wait, Boyehs," said my father, shaping each word patiently as if English were *his* native tongue and not the other way around. "Put away your hatcheks," he begged. "I have a key." He plucked at the fire chief's gold braid. "My aunt is at her daughter's house. We have holiday tonight."

Meanwhile, my stepmother, a pragmatist of the first water, had quietly snuck back into our house. To get her jewelry, she told me later, and to take the soup off the stove. Fire or no fire, we would need to eat eventually, and there was no point in letting the soup boil away.

"You'll have to get out of the way, sir," the chief said to my dad, stepping back to draw a proper bead on my aunt's front door. But my father planted himself firmly in front of Tante Leah's entrance to the two-flat, arms outstretched, looking for all the world like a man about to be crucified. I closed my eyes in embarrassment. Who knew what my father was capable of where birch doors were concerned? This was worse than my childhood, watching my mother publicly castigate the butcher for the state of his chickens, naming their shortcomings one by one.

Just then my stepmother appeared in Tante Leah's picture window, where she stood like a department store mannequin come to life. In either hand she held a silver candlestick with a candle guttering in each: the dancing light we had seen earlier. A murmur went up from the crowd, "Shabbos candles!" The chief tipped his helmet up on his forehead, shrugged, and turned his attention to the first floor once again.

My father held our front door open wide for the firemen, while my stepmother, I swear it, ran down from my aunt's flat to admonish each firefighter to wipe his feet. Behind them the men dragged a white hose uncoiling like a monumental tapeworm.

"Why does this night have to be different from all other nights?" I kept asking my husband, but he didn't answer me. In moments the retreat from our house began; firemen, hose, and chief emerged, followed by my stepmother wielding a broom. The disappointed crowd slowly dispersed to continue their respective seders and, at a wave from my father, we all trooped back into the house and took our seats again around the ping-pong table.

This time we had an extra guest, however, not Elijah, for whom the door is traditionally opened at each seder, but the fire chief himself, who said nervously, "Don't mind me. Go about your business and I'll see if I can't find your odor." For the smell of burning was still there, no question of it, and a pall of black smoke still hung above our heads.

So we found our places in the Haggadah, refilled our wineglasses, and were soon once more singing and chanting away, my father's yarmulke tilted rakishly over his forehead, my little brother sliding slowly off his chair. We had almost forgotten about the fire chief, for his reappearance about half an hour later startled us all. The singing trailed off weakly, and my little brother popped his head out from under the table to see if it was finally time to eat.

The chief bypassed my father and walked straight up to my stepmother as being, perhaps, the least crazy of the two. "Ma'am," he said respectfully enough, taking off his helmet and holding it over his chest, "are you people burning chickens here? Your odor smells like charred fowl feathers of some kind." At that my stepmother sprang from her chair, two coin-dots of color flushing her cheekbones.

"That's how pogroms get started," my husband muttered in my ear. Who knows what dimly remembered Passover conspiracies lay buried in my stepmother's consciousness? The chief might as well have come out and asked whether the matzos that crumbled on the table-cloth were made from the bones of little gentile boys.

"Come!" she said, grabbing the startled chief by his arm, drawing him into the tiny kitchen next to the recreation room. Stunned to silence, we could hear her rattling potlids. "Give a look, mister," she said. "Here is CHICKEN SOUP!" (Bang!) "Here is ROASTED CHICKEN!" (Bang!) "Here is PEAS WITH CAR-ROTS!" (Bang!) "This is AMERICA, mister. We are flicking here chickens in BUTCHER shop, not in the HOUSE!"

I thought about it later, how strange it all must have appeared to the chief: the group of us seated at the ping-pong table, the men in their yarmulkes, the candles, the bloodred wine, the blue-bound Haggadahs we seemed to be reading backwards, the seder plate with its shank bone and roasted egg, the chanting in Hebrew, and over all the mysterious insistent stink of something burning that had once been alive.

Years after, I learned that some people believe it is the terrible Blood Accusation (the charge that Jews drink Christian blood on Passover) that led Jews to open their doors during the seder, not to welcome Elijah as is com-monly thought, but to allay any suspicion on the part of gentile neighbors that secret practices were being fol-lowed inside.

As for *our* blood accusation, we discovered later in the evening that the smell of burning feathers was caused by a hapless pigeon that had fallen into our chimney and blocked it up.

All that was a long time ago. At the seders in my own house, we open the door for Elijah still. Sometimes in the silence that falls while we are waiting for him, I think I hear a soft flutter. But whether it is the sound of angel wings or merely pigeons flying—is another story.

THE DAY I BECAME A WOMAN, I took off my underpants with their scarlet stain and scrubbed them in the basement washtub. I wasn't versed in the ways of blood yet, didn't know how stubbornly it insists on telling secrets. The hot water I used only set the telltale blotches, and in desperation I finally threw the cotton pants into the furnace where they steamed and sizzled and threatened to quench the fire entirely.

We lived in Jackson, Michigan, then, in a gray stucco duplex we shared with an elderly Danish optometrist who collected stamps and saw his few patients in an office at the back of the house. Dr. Teters advertised his calling with a sign in the shape of a pair of spectacles on long legs poked into the bit of lawn on his side. He was one of the people I later tried to avoid, as I did all men who called themselves "Doctor," for I feared that with their scientific knowledge they might penetrate my secret more readily than ordinary males.

I LIKED OUR HOUSE, WITH ITS BEAUTIFUL WOODEN SLIDING doors that came out from between the walls to separate the front room and dining room. The staircase to the second floor was enclosed with a door behind which I could sit evenings when I was small and listen to adult conversation on the rare occasions my family gathered in the front room instead of the kitchen. My bedroom walls and gabled ceiling were papered in a rosy pattern with looped garlands, and from my window I could look out on the garden Dr. Teters grew: flowers whose English names my mother didn't know, Concord Blue grapes climbing on a white-painted arbor, a mulberry tree rank with fruit that dyed our fingers purple.

Hot summer nights when those gabled ceilings seemed to come down like the lids of hump-backed trunks, I dragged the sheet and pillow in my wake and took the stair treads, one by one, to find my people sleeping on the flowered carpet. I remember it all: my brother's eyelids twitching, the sea-scent from between my mother's thighs, my father's hand flung across her breast. We slept, sole to sole, our dreams pierced by streetcar clang, the leather slap of neighbors leaving for the factory's early shift, newsboys hawking extras: Amelia Earhart down in the Pacific.

"DO YOU REMEMBER FELIX?" MY FATHER SAYS. HE IS CARRY-
ing tools from the car to our basement, where he stores
them each night, his electric saw, his hammers and boxes
of nails. "Felix who used to work for me years ago in
Jackson? Felix who lived with us once when you were six
or seven? You remember him, don't you?"

Upstairs my mother listens to *The Goldbergs* as she
clatters potlids and puts the finishing touches to our supper. I can feel her shoes tramping back and forth on the
kitchen linoleum just above my head. For a moment I
am gripped with a terrible nostalgia for the tranquility my father has just shattered. His announcement has
plunged me back into a web from which I have been years
trying to extricate myself. I am fourteen, old enough
to look back on my time with Felix with a certain
amount of dispassion. I no longer believe, as I once did,
that certain seeds could lie in my body for years like
shriveled potatoes in a root cellar waiting for the right
combination of circumstances to sprout. I no longer have
the recurring dream in which a man with apple breasts
suckles a baby who becomes a wolf. This wolf, this false
baby, like the wolf-grandmother of Red Riding-
hood, wears a white cap tied under the chin with laces.
Always, at the end of the dream, the wolf-baby bites off
the father's breasts.

Nights when my parents were away—not yet back from Detroit, perhaps, where they had gone to visit relatives and bring back kosher meat, or simply playing cards a few blocks away at my aunt's house—I tossed on my bed making whirlpools of the sheets and blankets, picturing the cellar. Even today I can conjure up the cement walls, damp both winter and summer. In my mind, I walk the labyrinth of spaces: the laundry room first, ripe with bleach and bluing and un-washed clothes; the furnace room with a load of coal penned up behind a wooden barrier; the fruit shed, its shelves sagging under mason jars of pickled tomatoes and cucumbers, and beneath, on musty burlap sacks, softening apples and potatoes growing eyes. The dirtpacked floor is powdery under my bare feet; naked bulbs on chains hang from low beams interspersed with pipes and wires coiling in the shadows. Behind the furnace is the small room where Felix waits for me.

At supper my mother and father are unusually talkative. For once my mother does not call me "a regular Yankee" when I rearrange the cutlery she has placed on the table any which way. She calculates Felix's age by her own personal almanac: "I think he came to us the year we bought the Frigidaire. Didn't he watch you when we went for Bobbe's funeral?" Spearing a chunk of roasted beef from her own plate, she plops it on my father's plate and watches while he waves her hand away and then eats it. "Why, he must be over fifty now," she says, surprised, as if Felix is the only person in the world who has grown older.

My father keeps saying what a good-natured fellow Felix always was, how trustworthy even if he is a goy. He gets positively expansive about it; you would think his best friend is coming to visit instead of a guy who did odd jobs for him during the Depression and boarded with us a little while and whom, as far as I know, he hasn't seen or thought about in ages. On the other hand, *my* relationship to Felix isn't as easy to describe.

IN SEPTEMBER OF MY SIXTH GRADE YEAR, I WAS TRANSFERRED to the Pearl Street School, where, among other classes for children with special needs, I could attend "opportunity classes," a program reserved for students who were working ahead of their grade level. My Aunt Itkeh carried on about it, fussing with my hair and the Peter Pan collar of my red plaid dress. "They had to look all over town to find a school for her, that's how smart she is." "Too smart," my mother would say, making a great show of winking at her sister.

Those were pretty good times for me, a sixth grader lording it over the younger kids, in a state of grace at home because of my accomplishments at school. Dr. Teters gave me a lecture on the importance of education and then solemnly presented me with a special red and gold stamp with a crown on it honoring King Christian X of Denmark. To start my own collection, Dr. Teters said. Felix I pushed back into the compartment reserved for the unspeakable: images of Japanese soldiers bayoneting babies or fears that both my parents were going to die instantaneously in some random but inevitable cataclysm.

Early that first month of the transfer, I stood on a quiet street corner after school waiting for the crosstown bus, my canvas book bag fat with "A" papers for Mama in one hand, a lunch box in the other. The boy came out of nowhere, walking toward me, and the air was so still I could hear his corduroy knickers going whup, whup, and the dead brown oak leaves crunching under his high-top boots. Such a strange-looking boy: the no-color of maggots or the sole of your foot. No-color skin and no-color hair, only the eyes were pink and runny like those of some monstrous rabbit. And he looked up at me, squinting to shield his poor eyes from the slanting afternoon sun. "I'll tell you a joke," he said, "Mine is a wiener and yours is a bun."

UPSTAIRS, I PICK MY WAY THROUGH THE BEDROOM MY mother calls a *hegdesh*, a Jewish word I can't translate, but its meaning has always been perfectly clear to me. I put Mel Tormé on the record player and get a little pink around the earlobes remembering how my cousin Shirley and I were going to start a fan club for him and how I wrote him about it, saying I planned to have the motto be "Let's take the country by Torme," and how his secretary wrote back that it was a great idea, but the name was pronounced "Tor-*may*." I've got the volume turned way down, so I can hear the doorbell when Felix comes. Now I look at my flushed face in the mirror, consider a little pancake to tone it down. How will I look to him, I wonder. What will he say?

Felix moved out of our basement long before I moved to the Pearl Street School. We had Eileen O'Hara to stay with my brother and me when our parents were away. Sugar was scarce then because of the war, but whenever Eileen came she ignored my mother's instructions and cooked fudge. The house filled with the scent of melting sugar and cocoa and vanilla. Eileen told me she had read somewhere that young women in certain faraway countries put vanilla behind their ears instead of perfume. I imagined girls in flower necklaces and Dorothy Lamour sarongs luring their golden lovers with skin that smelled of Hershey bars.

Eileen plucked her eyebrows with a little pair of metal tweezers and polished her toenails, placing pledgets of cotton between her toes. Mostly she sat next to the telephone waiting for her boyfriend, George, to call.

She would grasp the candlestick phone by its handles, lift the receiver, and hold down the cradle with one finger so she could release it the very second George rang. As the moments of anticipation went by and the silence in the house grew palpable, I could feel my heart ticking like a wind-up alarm, giddy with the sweet fudge melting in my mouth and my love of her love for George.

We girls at the Pearl Street School collected paper dolls cut from the Sunday comics, mostly *Boots*, *Tillie the Toiler*, and *Fritzie Ritz*. We put each set between the leaves of Montgomery Ward or Sears catalogues and our teacher allowed us to keep them in the supply cupboard where she stored the construction paper, scissors, and gallon jars of white, sweet-smelling paste. She let us take the books out at recess on days it rained or at lunchtime if we lived too far away to go home.

Because I was one of the few students who lived on the other side of town, I often played with my paper dolls while I ate the salami sandwich my mother packed and the bottle of pop I bought cold from the cooler of a nearby confectionary. All the children who lunched at school were given bottles of milk for which our parents paid a small fee each year. This milk caused me much anguish because, of course, I was not able to drink it with my sandwich. Sometimes I considered explaining to my teacher that for me mixing milk and meat was a sin, but that would have meant so much other explanation that I simply hid the bottle in my desk, and when no one was around, smuggled it into the lavatory and poured the milk down a toilet. I say "simply," but that wasn't always the case. Some days my classroom was never empty, and the toilet stalls had no doors, so there were weeks when the bottles of milk collected in my desk, turned to cheese, and began to stink.

There was more. At first I played with my own paper dolls, laying out the sets on my desk, dressing the different dolls in suits and coats and hats, imagining social gatherings at which they met and conversed. But then I began pulling out other catalogues and leafing through them to see what new dolls other girls had managed to find. Some girls had grandparents who sent them cutouts from papers in other cities. Their catalogues bulged with so many dolls that the leaves gaped open. When I grew bolder, I took the books to my desk and made up elaborate combinations in which my dolls and those that belonged to the other girls interacted in a way that did not happen in my real life.

One day I slipped a set of *Boots* cutouts from the catalogue of a popular girl named Nancy Piper and placed them in my own book. I told myself she had plenty of dolls, far more than she needed, that I deserved them more than she. While moments before I took the cutouts, the schoolroom had seemed to be filled with a silence thick as cotton batting, now it seemed to collect every particle of sound from every cubicle of the building's spaces. I felt I could hear the blind children tracing their fingertips over the blistered surfaces of their Braille readers, the sandpaper rasp of the asthmatics in the open-air classes as they struggled for breath, the fluttering gestures of the children we called deaf and dumb. But the fragile dolls became mine, and though I waited and waited, no one seemed to miss them at all.

I took more dolls from different collections until my own catalogue bulged in the middle, until its leaves splayed out in a fan. Each time I went to the cupboard, I felt invincible—better yet, invisible, as if no one could stop me because I was someone they could not see. Then one day Miss Highlar called a special assembly to say in a soft trembling voice that something shocking was happening in the opportunity class of the Pearl Street School.

Even before we filed into our seats, the boys through one door, the girls through another, I knew what Miss Highlar was going to tell us. I sat listening to her with my hands folded on my desk as we had been taught to do, my face tight as wax, heard her talking about respecting what belonged to other people, keeping your hands to yourself, doing only things you would want your parents to know about. I wanted to put my fingers in my ears as I did on the Fourth of July to blunt the thunderclap of fireworks, but I kept my fingers laced as if in prayer. The room smelled of the cleaning compound our janitor pushed ahead of his long broom and of tomato soup from lunchtime thermoses. Around me, my classmates sat behind their desks, the girls with their legs primly together, the boys opening and closing their knickers like pairs of scissors. I was certain Miss Highlar had discovered my secret, that before she dismissed my classmates she would tell them all about me and what I had done with Felix.

WHEN THE DOORBELL FINALLY RINGS, I DON'T DO MY USUAL stampede routine, knocking over anyone who happens to be in my way in case it's one of my friends who will die of embarrassment at having to deal with my parents or my obnoxious brothers. In fact, for a moment I've forgotten who's coming at all. And then I do remember, and stand so quickly the blood rushes to my head and I feel faint enough to sit back down again.

"I'm coming, I'm coming," I shout down the stairs, trying to keep my voice ladylike, not easy to do when you're screaming your head off. My father is waiting at the bottom, just about to call me again. "Where are you?" he asks impatiently. "Felix wants to see you." It's my dad who wants to see me. This show can't go on without me.

I can tell that the second I walk into the living room and see my mother plucking at the gold braid on our new pale blue damask sofa where she sits, silently, across from an equally silent old man I can barely recognize.

"What do you think of our girl?" my father says. "She's a regular young lady now." Felix's eyes brush over me a moment and then return to the battered tan fedora, the brim of which he keeps turning in his hands like a steering wheel. His baggy white-on-white dress shirt tucks into trousers that bunch over his small pot but are short enough to reveal black garters holding up his ankle socks. "A regular young lady," he agrees, twirling the hat.

My mother pats the cushion next to her. "Sit by me," she says, and puts her arm around my shoulders in a way she hasn't done in years. Is this protection or proprietorship; I don't know. One part of me blushes, stutters, feels the silk at the back of my knees, and my mother's arm, a yoke, holding me still. They are talking about the old days now, and the names, the places, like a little sand toy I had once had, dig down, scoop, come up, tip out, dig down again until I am back in that cellar, the dirt floor cold and gritty under the soles of my feet.

It was to be our secret; "Cross your heart and hope to die," Felix told me, at a time when that oath had not yet lost the purity and impact of its intent. There in that damp little room, the cast-off Axminster on the floor, short windows at the top shrouded in burlap bags, coal dust seeping, we played out the small drama whose lines and movements I would soon know by heart.

The army cot covered by a lumpy quilt stands against a wall, a wooden orange crate set on end next to it, holding a crumpled pack of Kools and a *Popular Detective* magazine. Its cover depicts a wide-eyed blonde girl, her blouse ripped off one shoulder, a black revolver to her temple.

A leather razor strop hangs from a nail on one wall, near the round mirror. Underneath sits another orange crate that holds a straight razor and a brush sitting in a china shaving mug painted with tiny blue flowers and the motto Forget-me-not. He tells me stories, Felix, of children lost in dark woods, orphans and stepmothers, grandmothers who dress like wolves, or is it the other way around?

Somehow he makes me understand that what goes on here must not escape this room. Terrible trouble will come if I tell, and that burden rests on my shoulders like a heavy arm. He sits holding me on his lap in an old easy chair, its coil springs poking through the sheet that drapes it, petting me, telling me those things, the whiskey on his breath whirling in my head. And always his hands and that rearing snake, its one sad eye weeping, weeping.

"So, Felix," says my father, "would you like something to drink? A whiskey?" I can feel my mother's arm stiffen with disapproval. "Don't mind if I do," Felix replies, crossing and uncrossing his long legs. We wait silently while my father goes to get the drinks. I tell myself I'm not angry with this poor disgusting bum, for that's what he is; the Salvation Army clothes are easy to spot and so is the sunken jaw no dentist has tended to in years. Still I haven't the nerve to stare at him, to force him to meet my eyes, to remind him of our conspiracy if he has been able to forget it. I have only to get him out of my head now, where he never had any right to be in the first place. What's the damage, after all? What did he take from me but my childhood?

My father comes back into the living room with a bottle of Seagram's Seven Crown and two shot glasses. He pours two drinks to the rims of the little glasses. "To old times," he says, taking a tiny sip and then tossing down the rest. "To old friends," says Felix.

IN A SEVENTH GRADE ENGLISH class we are reading silently the last page of Steinbeck's *Of Mice and Men*. For days we have been discussing the symbiotic relationship of George and Lennie, the elements in each man that support the other in a world where loneliness is symbolized by the disparate characters gathered in the bunkhouse of an isolated ranch.

I watch my students' faces as they visualize the final scene: the two men hiding in the brush, the menacing footsteps approaching, Lennie's eyes fixed on the distant mountains. "We're gonna get this place," says George, beginning the now-familiar litany, and I know my students have inferred already what happens to the best-laid plans. "Le's do it now. Le's get that place now," Lennie begs as George raises the gun behind him. I hold my breath, waiting, reliving my own first encounter with that book, the hot spurt of tears, and dreams shattered by a pistol shot that rolls up the hills and down again.

One by one the children finish, subdued, moved,

impatient for their classmates to catch up so we can talk about it, seduced once again by that most golden of pleasures—a good book.

You might wonder how a group of today's twelve-year-olds can connect with two itinerant barley buckers from the Depression. The risk I run, exposing them to material supposedly beyond their grasp, is developing in these youngsters a lifelong aversion to any book, good or bad. Well, I guess I decided long ago that kids learn to read by reading, and if that is so, why not let them read the best literature we have to offer?

In fact, "Becoming a Nation of Readers," the 1985 report of the Commission on Reading, suggests that "the pace of instruction strongly predicts year-to-year gains in reading." The report goes on to say that "children of any given level of ability who are in fast-paced groups show growth beyond the expected." I don't find all this revolutionary. Any of my old English teachers could have predicted these findings.

Ernest Hemingway had not yet written *The Old Man and the Sea* when I was in seventh grade in 1942 and my own English teacher was force-feeding us books. But if he had, she probably would have made us read it. She loved Hemingway and Dickens and Melville and Shakespeare, and she trusted her instincts and her students enough to assign them material she felt wouldn't insult them.

We read *Oliver Twist* that year, and I can still remember following the tortuous plot as it twisted and turned like the very streets of London Dickens described. I went on to devour *Dombey and Son* and *Great Expectations* the summer I was thirteen, hefting great armloads of books home from the public library, selecting by sheer weight sometimes, begrudging each turned page because it brought me closer to the end.

One crisp Michigan winter evening, I heard Lionel Barrymore read *A Christmas Carol* on the radio, and for the first time I felt myself connected to a community of readers like myself—who knew how many—people as numerous as the stars that glittered above the snug house in which I followed the familiar words.

Shakespeare? Some benighted English teacher made me memorize huge chunks of it in eighth grade: *Hamlet*, *Macbeth*, *Romeo and Juliet*. "Is this a dagger which I see before me . . . ?" I learned those lines and have them today when traffic stalls on Connecticut Avenue or when too much coffee keeps me dancing on my bed at night.

Of course there were long passages we didn't understand: references, allusions, symbols. That's what our English teacher was for. Like a magician, she could pull verbal rabbits out of a seemingly empty line of prose or poetry. She was our tour guide, our decoder, our tastemaker. Few of us snapped from being stretched. I think the greater danger, always, was growing flabby from *lack* of tension.

We were the children of shopkeepers and factory workers. Many of our parents had never finished high school; some of them, like mine, didn't speak English at home. I don't recall having a book of my own until I entered kindergarten, but once within the schoolhouse walls, I got the idea of reading quickly enough. Who could have resisted the bait?

There in our gaily decorated schoolroom, we moved at an orchestrated pace that felt to us as natural as the sunlight that flooded our windows. Simulated forts and cabins grew under our hands from piles of great wooden blocks. We fought to be mother or father in the playhouse with its child-sized furniture and cunning little pots and pans. Swathed in our fathers' old shirts turned back-to-front, we stood at easels dipping fat brushes into jars of bright color, as the yellow suns we painted in the corners of pictures dripped down the page toward the houses and grass and flowers. It seems to me now as I look back that we moved in a slow-motion, dreamlike way, pretending, imagining, unaware that we were getting ready for that most miraculous of human accomplishments: learning to read.

My own students come to me from differing backgrounds. Some were public school children; some have attended other private schools. Some read everything from cereal boxes to sci-fi trilogies; others read nothing but *TV Guide*. They are like what the poet Gerard Manley Hopkins celebrates, "dappled things," in various stages of reading ability. Before the school year is out, all of them will read Steinbeck, Poe, Wilder, O. Henry, Twain, and more, some of the best of our literature.

As my own teachers did, I read to my students. Even seventh graders will stop bouncing off walls when a story is on the agenda. And if you think a twelve-year-old is too sophisticated to be read to, come visit my classroom some day. I set the stage first, of course, with a preview of coming attractions to establish a context: a short biography of the author and a bit about the setting. Then, as the students follow along in their own texts, I tune them in to each author's individual voice and rhythms. Together we take leisurely digressions comparing the work we are reading to others we may know or to similar experiences we may have had.

Because I am reading to them, I am there to answer questions when they arise and to ask a few of my own. We keep a dictionary handy. Importantly, I know when to stop. All those years of Saturday matinee serials stand me in good stead. Just when I know by the rapt silence that every last child is hooked, I say, "Okay, finish the chapter for homework." And they do, and come to homeroom the next morning to argue about just what happened.

To deny students exposure to classics for fear they are not ready for them is to consign them to books that may entertain but never challenge. Further, we take the chance that in a world of business courses and computer curriculums, they may never get pushed out of the Judy Blume womb at all.

As to the risk that young people will not understand every level of a given classic, where is it written that we need read the best in literature only once in a lifetime? That's like saying, "I don't want to visit Paris again; I've already been there."

I'VE BEEN THINKING A LOT
about repairs lately; so much in the world needs fixing.
Setting things right seemed easier once. "Here," my
mother says, unwinding a length of pink thread from its
spool. Looping it around her cupped fingers, she breaks
off the rosy skein with a snap. "Chew the piece of thread
I gave you and be quiet," she tells me. I lean my weight
from foot to foot, wary of her needle but anxious to be out
once more with my friends. "Hurry, Ma!" "Don't talk,"
she says. "How many time do I have to tell you? Chew
the thread or the devil will sew up your wits along with
this tear." She points to the long ruffle she is accordion-
pleating back onto the skirt of my sunsuit. I am five years
old, and sewed-up wits or not, there is little in my world
my mother cannot mend with her needle or my father
with his hammer and saw.

Today it's 10:30 in the morning, not one of my days at
the university, so I have the privilege of staying home and
listening to Gus and his rainbow coalition of workmen

stomp around on my third floor trying to deal with walls that have gone twenty years without a paint job. Now that I've resigned myself to the certainty that none of my four kids is coming home to stay, I'm eager to break up the shrines and toss all the relics they refuse to take to their own homes.

So the Day Sleeper sign gets pried off Frank's door. I had a terrible pang about the crayoned scrawl that said, "This is Seth's room. Please ASK to use my stereo," but fortunately Gus got to it before I totally lost my sense of proportion. No problem with Lizzy's purple ceiling: the only one who mourned that was Frenchy, who needed three coats of paint to cover it. Gus is yelling at Frenchy now the way people do when they speak to foreigners. "Eh, Frenchy, you spackle dis wall good, eh?" If hollering won't get through, then perhaps pidgin English will.

I'm not supposed to be listening to all this; I've got work to do. And I'm not supposed to be nostalgic about old Beatles posters or shoe boxes full of baseball cards, either. The sense of loss I sometimes still feel about our boomingly empty house is natural and finite—reparable. What came in the mail earlier today has ripped the fabric of my life in a way that won't mend without showing. "You asked what the doctors said about my losing forty pounds," my friend Terry writes. "I didn't have the nerve to tell you (because of the stigma), but I want to tell you now for I feel close enough to you; you are like a sister. Faye, I have AIDS."

At my kitchen table, surrounded by the homely scent of perked coffee, the dailiness of scattered newspapers and empty cereal bowls, I mechanically plow through the rest of the mail: the gas bill, the PepCo bill, a postcard from my brother, an invitation to a political fundraiser I ought to attend. My friend is thirty-two years old—younger than three of my own children. He is an artist, gifted, poised at that shimmering moment when promise has grabbed hold and taken root. And now this.

Terry has asked me to look into facilities for AIDS victims in DC. He is too lonely where he is, too fearful of revealing his condition to seek help in his small town, if there *is* help. I am happy to do something. Trailing the coiled telephone cord behind me, I rinse coffee cups and brush off bread crumbs while people named Charlotte and Harold and Rusty speak to me calmly, listen while I tell Terry's story over and over. Sadly, what I have to say is not new to them. Someone at the Whitman Walker Clinic gives me the number for the AIDS Hotline: 332-AIDS. I'm struck by how institutionalized all this already is. "Tell your friend to come to Washington," the young man at the other end of the hotline says. "We have a buddy program, and there are group housing opportunities for people in his situation." I want to ask him if he, too, has AIDS, and if he is afraid, but of course I don't. I've been around long enough not to breach the etiquette of hotlines; I understand about anonymity and how it works both ways.

Now I have pages of notes, something to give Terry so the letter I write him won't simply be filled with words too frail to carry my horror and my grief. Terry is a dead man. "I'm sorry" seems a ridiculous response. But there is no end to how ghastly this all is. Terry's envelope lies unopened on my kitchen table. When I reach for it to copy the return address, my hand stops in midair. Terry sealed that envelope, didn't he? He must have sealed it with his tongue. "You're an idiot," I tell myself in disgust. "You know better." But in the bathroom, I wash my hands over and over again, cursing myself for the coward I am, understanding for a brief, blinding flash just what Terry's loneliness really means.

Gus's bulk fills the doorway of my office. I have important decisions to make about the relative merits of "warm beige" or "antique white," and whether that old bunk bed in Frank's room goes or stays. I shudder away the image of Frank, a five-year-old, sitting on the bottom bunk burning with a fever we will learn is meningitis. The other kids and Jack still claim he is my favorite, tease me about it. How do I explain he is a new son, given me twice, one of God's too few second chances, and yes, I am not insensible of that gift. Still, that was thirty years ago. "Chuck the bed," I tell Gus, sickened by my reluctance to let go of things. "No problem," he says.

WHEN I WAS A CHILD, I FOL-
lowed avidly a radio program called *Court of Missing Heirs* where thousands of dollars in unclaimed legacies were announced on the air. Week after week, I listened for my name to be called, convinced with the egocentricity of the very young that somewhere a long-lost, fabulously wealthy relative had died with my name on his lips, and that it remained only for his executors to find me in my little Michigan town and change my life forever.

I've been a grown woman for a long time now; I no longer dream of winning the lottery, and my chances for financial inheritance are slim. Nevertheless, I've been thinking a lot about legacies lately. After years of despairing that our baby-boom children would ever decide they were old enough to have babies of their own, we are finally grandparents. Now we find ourselves projecting the future by how old we will be when Baby Helen goes to kindergarten or whether we will have to use walkers to dance at Baby Henry's wedding. Suddenly each passing year takes on an additional sharpness honed by our desire to share and affect the sweet unfolding of their lives.

Still, the candles with which we attempt to peer down the dim corridors of what's to come gutter feebly against the dark. And so we found ourselves, my husband and I, sitting in a lawyer's office not too long ago, revising the will we had not looked at or thought about since our four children were small and our major concern had been who we would trust to raise them if we both should suddenly die in an auto crash or some other unthinkable disaster.

While we spoke of bequests and net worth and executors, I glanced at my husband, thought of how for forty years we had worked side by side putting together the estate whose division we were now discussing. To us, both children of the Depression, of parents who had come to America with little more than featherbeds and their treasured Sabbath candlesticks, the figures we were now bandying around seemed impressive.

I remembered how my mother-in-law had purchased an insurance policy long ago for our eldest daughter, Shoshana, her first grandchild. Twenty-five cents a week went into a coffee tin so Grandma could give the insurance agent the dollar payment he collected monthly at her door. Almost eighteen years later, when both the policy and the granddaughter had matured, Shoshana received the two hundred and fifty dollars that Grandma had hoped would pay for college clothes.

I looked out the window of the attorney's office to see in the distance the slim finger of the Washington Monument pointing toward the sky, admonishing me. The entire legal discussion seemed so earthbound to me, so sterile, so far from my real concerns for my children. Who could foretell what difference our savings would one day make in their lives or in the lives of their children? Was there an inflation-proof method of ensuring their happiness? Testaments and beneficiaries, codicils and clauses . . . I was pierced suddenly by the thought of a world in which I no longer existed. Who would console my children when they lost their mother, if I was not there to do it?

I thought back to a sun-drenched day in Michigan almost half a century before. I saw us all so clearly, my mother and father safely young again, my two little brothers not yet grown—my family—gamboling in a lake so pure the sun reached down to dapple small stones on its wrinkled sand floor. From a wicker basket covered with a snowy linen towel, my mother gave us sandwiches wrapped in waxed paper and bright red cherries we had bought from a farmer on the road. Skin prickling with the sunburn that would keep us all awake that night, we ate and laughed, and perhaps it was that uncommon light that did it, but the memory was etched so deeply that even this moment I know the taste of cherries in my mouth, feel my father's bare arm against my own.

Driving home from the lawyer's office, my husband and I were quiet, locked into our own thoughts. Perhaps the sense of finality that accompanies wills and lawyers discourages small talk; I was still mulling a medium of exchange that has nothing to do with money. "I wish you would give up smoking," my husband said, finally. I knew what he had really meant to say.

WE WENT ON VACATION SHORTLY AFTER THAT AND WHEN WE returned our son Frank called me from Columbus, Ohio, where he's been living for years, though to look at the baseball cards and tattered sports magazines piled up in his old room, you'd think he might still be coming down to dinner every night.

"I missed you guys while you were gone," Frank said, his voice crackling over the long distance wires. "Especially one night when I took the dog out for a walk around ten o'clock. For some reason it seemed like every house or so people were sitting on the lawn, mothers and fathers on blankets and their kids nearby. All you could hear were the sounds of voices, a car going by once in a while, and the crickets, loud like they are this time of year." He went on. "I thought how strange it was for so many kids to be up right then. I asked myself what they were all doing outside way after dark on a weekday evening."

Listening, delight began to well up in me. With absolute certainty, as if I were hearing a familiar story, I anticipated the explanation. Like a child, I could hardly resist shouting out the final lines. And more than that, I knew *why* Frank was telling me this particular tale. But having raised four children, I have learned to be patient, and so I waited for my son to tell me what I had already figured out.

"I kept walking," Frank said, "and saw more people, and after a while I realized that this was the night of a lunar eclipse, and all those families were sitting out there waiting to see it together. That's when I wanted to call you and Dad. I remembered you waking us up in the middle of the night and wrapping us in blankets so we could go outside to watch the moon disappear and then come back again. That's when I really missed you. I wished you were home so I could call you and tell you I remembered."

We've tucked the will away in a fire-proofed box, the way people do with important papers. But in the meantime I keep building equity. Each Saturday Baby Helen comes over and we play "this little piggy" and "the eensie beensie spider." I hold her in my arms and sing to her, "Hush little baby, don't say a word," just as I sang it to her mother. When she spends the night, we get up early and sit on the front porch so we can listen to the birds as I did when her Aunt Lizzie was small. Helen's grandfather takes her for walks up to Wisconsin Avenue and on the way he tells her the names of trees and points out the squirrels who live in them. Each time we see her, we make another deposit in her memory bank.

Baby Henry lives in Manhattan. We have promised ourselves that we will try to see him once a month. One day when he is a little older, I want to show him how to write a book of his own; I'll bring out the one I helped his father make on an afternoon when he was small and rain kept us prisoner. Some day when Henry wants to try his wings and his parents hover a bit too closely, maybe I'll remind them of the time we drove his father to a place just outside of Charlottesville, where he started a solo bicycle trip across the country. Maybe I'll tell them then of the tears we waited to shed until after he had pedaled off. And maybe, if we're not around to do it, Henry's father will tell the story himself, and in the remembering have the courage to let go of his son.

Of course I hope we will be able to put by a financial nest egg for our children; no memory of food ever appeased hunger. But whatever happens, we will go on practicing our other, more sublime economy, one that will never be of the faintest interest to the IRS. I suspect those are the investments that will keep paying dividends to our children and grandchildren long after we are gone.

I NEVER STOP BELIEVING I'LL find something worth keeping at a yard sale. Years of sorting through dusty depressing plastic flower arrangements and mismatched crazed crockery have failed to dampen my bargain hunter's spirit. Among those impossible lamps a genuine Tiffany just might be hiding; somewhere in this world there exists a Rip Van Winkle type who doesn't yet know what an old patchwork quilt is worth.

That's why one lazy summer day out in the Virginia countryside where we have had a weekend place for years I cruised the backroads in search of the perfect yard sale. The professional-looking signs that alerted me a half mile down the road, and eventually the house itself, a substantial brick rambler, gave promise of some better-than-average pickings, so I parked my car on the shoulder and made my way over the grass, past two rusty power lawn mowers and a reel mower (for sale), and a white-painted tire planted with purple and white petunias (not for sale).

I felt wonderful, the scent of a potential bargain making blood sing in my ears. Leisurely, I circled the two aluminum folding tables that had been set up to display a toaster, a set of electric hair-curlers, a box of hairnets in their original individual packages, assorted greeting cards, children's clothing, plastic toys, *Readers Digest* condensed books, and Cozzens' ubiquitous *By Love Possessed*—in short, the usual yard sale fare. But that pitcher holding some kitchen gadgets might have been handmade. It was just ugly enough to be interesting, with its leaf-green base that burst into a crown of violet flowers at the lip and rim. Definitely a possibility. And what about that chenille bedspread, sporting a peacock with his trailing tail outlined in yellow and pink and lime-green art deco colors. Wasn't it so hideous it might be fun?

Mentally, I put on my shrewd bargain hunter's cap, prepared to be ruthless in my dickering with whichever of the three gray-haired women sitting in plastic lawn chairs claimed ownership of either item. "Y'all live around here?" one of the women asked, approaching me. "Boston," I replied, naming the little village where we get our country mail. "Washington?" she said, not hearing me, but I insisted on establishing my local credentials so I said "Boston" again, "Boston, Virginia." In moments she had me pegged, had located our farm, knew the people from whom we had bought it years before, told me her name—Dolly Corbin. We began jabbering away about nothing: the weather, how various garden crops were doing—the polite ceremonial talk before money is exchanged in the country.

And then my would-be saleslady was distracted by a small verbal exchange between one of the other women and a tall beefy man in Bermuda shorts and a loud Hawaiian shirt. I began looking in my purse. The asking price for the pitcher was four dollars; the spread was marked eight. Ten dollars seemed like a good price to offer for both items.

"Oh, no," the woman was telling Bermuda Shorts, and the third woman called out from her perch on the lawn chair, "What's he tryin' to do?" The tall man grinned sheepishly and said, "Wal, you're *supposed* to bargain at a sale." By this time they were all getting into the act. Dolly wiggled her tight gray curls, fresh from the beauty parlor. "You ain't a Jew, are you?" she asked playfully, looking the man up and down. "You're acting like a Jew, tryin' to jew her down!"

Now I ask myself why I didn't just turn around and walk back across the lawn and down the narrow highway shoulder to my car. I could have let them all put two and two together, as they say around there. I didn't need to become Mrs. Sixties Relevant again. But I was angry about my sweet day suddenly turned sour. Only the week before I had read a front-page article in the *Washington Post* that said Polish peasants remained stubbornly anti-Semitic, that the prejudice was in their folk culture, in their bones. "Who in hell have they got to be anti-Semitic about?" I had shouted at my poor husband, who was hidden behind his section of the morning paper. "The Polish Jews are all dead anyhow."

SHORTLY AFTER MY HUSBAND AND I MARRIED, WE MOVED to Oak Park, a new suburb of Detroit. There we helped form a local Democratic club and joined the county Democratic party in hopes of purging it of the Teamsters, who dominated the organization then. With others we formed a liberal/labor caucus and in a surprisingly short time I was chairman of our city club, while my husband was persuaded to run for state representative. We wore a track down Woodward Avenue, driving back and forth to Pontiac, the county seat, for meetings.

Our county chairman was an old party hack, amiable enough, a local businessman who had been around Democratic politics forever. Whatever he thought about the influx of young couples from Detroit, he must have realized that we were there to stay. So he patiently put up with our naiveté, our often sanctimonious insistence on being issue-oriented, our stuffy nitpicking to the tune of Robert's Rules. And we in our turn looked to the aging party bosses as relics from another time, with the same fascinating but distant relationship to us as the old iceboxes that still sat in our parents' garages in Detroit or the washboards in their basements.

Though we were drawn to the rich lode of political lore the old pols possessed, we often found the atmosphere in the smoke-filled rooms stifling. How could we fail to notice the patronizing way our chairman spoke to the few blacks who belonged to the party, or ignore his calling them "darkies" behind their backs; how many times could we listen to him brag about "buying low and selling high" in one breath and "jewing 'em down" in the next? My husband and I had long, very serious discussions about whether it would do any good to speak to Calvin. "He doesn't really mean anything by it," is what my husband said. "It's habit . . . automatic, part of the local dialect. And anyway, he won't change."

Whether Calvin's attitudes were mere convention or not, they wormed at me, caused anger to burrow away somewhere deep inside. In the first place we weren't all that comfortable yet about being Jews in Oakland County. Perhaps we remembered how rigidly the lakes had been segregated out there: this one for Jews, that one Christians only. For all I knew, protective covenants were still the order of the day; real estate agents were simply more discreet about it than before.

Nevertheless I couldn't let it go. One evening I managed to get my chairman alone for a moment before a county committee meeting. "Calvin," I said, taking a deep breath, "I know you don't mean anything by it," lying through my teeth, "but some of us are upset by certain ways you have of putting things. Now you and I both know it's just a way of speaking. Still, I thought I'd sort of remind you that saying 'jew 'em down' and 'darkie' really offends people. You're the Democratic county chairman; you're supposed to set an example." Calvin looked at me with the same degree of concern as if I had just told him he'd picked up the wrong fork at the Dairy Workers' banquet. "Honey," he said, "nobody pays any attention to stuff like that. You're too sensitive."

By that time I was sorry I had bothered to bring the matter up at all. We walked into the meeting together, Calvin's arm around my shoulders. He did everything but give me a conciliatory pat on the rear. During the course of the meeting, Calvin made a progress report on his negotiations for the building where we were to have our county convention. "We're still some dollars apart on the price of the extra caucus rooms," Calvin said, "but I think we can jew 'em down a little more." Then he looked at me from over his half-glasses. "No offense, Faye," he said. That was consciousness-raising in the fifties.

SLOWLY DOLLY CORBIN CAME BACK INTO FOCUS. "LOOK," I said to her. "Look . . ." finding it difficult to break into the conversation, as if it were enclosed in a membrane. "I was going to make an offer on that spread there. You're supposed to bargain at a yard sale; everyone knows that. It has nothing to do with being a Jew, though I happen to be one. People like a good buy. That's why they come to yard sales in the first place."

And all the while I was delivering my speech, Dolly Corbin was slowly backing away from me. Recoiling is what it was; I don't know any other way to describe it. "I was just kiddin' him," she said, pale suddenly except for the patchy rouge on her cheeks. "I didn't mean anything by it." Of course I felt instantly sorry for her, sorry I'd made a fuss; still something in me made me push on. "But we can't keep doing that to each other," I said. "Just because someone wants the best price doesn't make him a Jew. I'll bet you don't even know any Jews!"

"I didn't mean anything by it," Dolly said again with a strange small smile. "We was all kiddin' around." "But you hurt people," I insisted, surprised at the old pain welling up in me, the prickling in my nose, the sudden tears. "You hurt people, and you say you don't mean it, but you keep on doing it."

I turned and walked back to my car, conscious of Mrs. Corbin's "I'm sorry" trailing after me. "Yeah, you're sorry all right, sorry you lost a sale, you old bag," I muttered, just plain angry now, sick of the stereotypes, the assumption behind her remarks that everyone felt as she did, that she could say what she did as she probably had all her life without anyone calling her on it. On top of it all, I felt suddenly vulnerable. Dolly Corbin knew who I was, where I lived. Why had I made such a scene about being Jewish? Now she would send her redneck relatives to burn crosses in front of our house.

Driving back to our farm, I hardly noticed the Queen Anne's lace trimming the selvages of the fields, the patches of bright blue chickory and wild oxeye daisies everywhere. The day was ruined for me. I kept thinking that forty years had gone by since I argued with Calvin about the same kind of "harmless" labeling, and nothing had really changed except that Calvin was long dead and I was now as old as he was then.

This morning's *Post* carries an article with the dateline of Obergammergau, West Germany, where a passion play has been produced every ten years or so since the early seventeenth century. According to the story, Obergammergau residents are angry with Jews who boycotted the passion play in 1970 and who continue to claim that parts of the six-hour play about the life of Christ are anti-Semitic. The article goes on to say that surveys show that there remains in Germany "a firmly anti-Semitic core of 15 percent." So what else is new?

Driving around in a circle on Connecticut Avenue later in the morning, I pass two young women in picture hats waving picket signs from the sidewalk. Their placards read, "Free Tibet." The front pages are so crowded with bad news I have to maneuver the circle twice before the message registers. Free Tibet? Get serious, guys. What makes you think anyone will notice you in your silly hats, and more than that, what makes you think that anyone has time to worry about yet another injustice?

The funny thing is, I keep thinking about the women and their signs, and when I go around the circle one last time, they dip those placards at me once again. Free Tibet? Well, why not. Thumbs up, I say, sticking my hand out the window. It isn't much, but you can't believe how good that makes me feel.

The Feminist Press is an independent nonprofit literary publisher that promotes freedom of expression and social justice. We publish exciting writing by women and men who share an activist spirit and a belief in choice and equality. Founded in 1970, we began by rescuing "lost" works by writers such as Zora Neale Hurston and Charlotte Perkins Gilman, and established our publishing program with books by American writers of diverse racial and class backgrounds. Since then we have also been bringing works from around the world to North American readers. We seek out innovative, often surprising books that tell a different story.

See our complete list of books at **feministpress.org**, and join the Friends of FP to receive all our books at a great discount.

THE FEMINIST PRESS
AT THE CITY UNIVERSITY OF NEW YORK
FEMINISTPRESS.ORG